A LAUGH A DAY

"Laugh if you want to stay healthy," my doctor once advised me. "Life needs a balance. It can't be all one way or all the other."

I wasn't convinced.

"Laugh?" I demurred. "With problems like inflation, the energy crunch, and taxes? Especially taxes. Who can afford such luxury!"

"How can anyone not afford it?" was the medico's response.

"You don't understand, doctor," I said. "I just don't have time. There are other things that absolutely have to be done. Serious things."

"What's more serious than your life?" he challenged.

Rx
FOR HILARITY

Dr. Abraham Unger

BELMONT TOWER BOOKS • NEW YORK CITY

A TOWER BOOK

Published by

Tower Publications, Inc.
Two Park Avenue
New York, N.Y. 10016

Rx
FOR HILARITY

FOREWORD

"Laugh if you want to stay healthy," my doctor once advised me. "Life needs a balance. It can't be all one way or all the other."

I wasn't convinced.

"Laugh?" I demurred. "With problems like inflation, energy crunches and taxes? Especially taxes. Who can afford such luxury!"

"How can anyone not afford it?" was the medico's response.

"You don't understand, doctor," I said. "I just don't have time. There are other things that absolutely have to be done. Serious things."

"What's more serious than your life?" he challenged.

"Nice going, doctor," I complimented, "but I still have to meet bills and support a family. Just to exist these days takes money and lots of it."

"Granted," he agreed, "but tell me, how much does it cost you to laugh?"

That one stopped me. But good.

"Nothing," I had to admit. "Not a single dime."

"And no sales tax either," he added.

That made it sound even better and after some thought I realized he was right. Laughter relaxed me and brightened up my days. And my nights too. It made my life a gourmet meal instead of merely a regular dinner.

Below are some of the chuckles that gave me a wonderful lift. Try them on for size. If they don't fit, what have you lost?

JANUARY 1

"Please, Uncle George," the young tyke begged, "please make a noise like a frog."

"Whatever for?" asked the amazed relative.

"Because," explained the lad, "every time I ask Daddy for something expensive he tells me to wait until my rich Uncle George croaks."

JANUARY 2

A stern father told his sixteen year old daughter that the morals of today's generation were extremely lax and to prove his point he said, "Girls of today don't blush anymore regardless of what you say to them. When I was young it was different."

"Gosh, Father," exclaimed the surprised daughter, "what did you say to them?"

JANUARY 3

A lion once caught a bull and ate it. The meal was so delicious that he roared his enjoyment to all corners of the jungle. A nearby hunter, attracted by the noise, found the lion an easy mark and killed the beast with one well aimed shot. The moral of the story is that when you're full of bull—shut up.

JANUARY 4

Tipping the porter handsomely the groom cautioned him not to reveal the newly married status of his bride and himself. The next morning, though, he was annoyed by angry glances from the other passengers on the train and he called the porter to account.

"No, sir," insisted the porter. "I never told anyone you were married. A few people asked me but I only said that you were good friends."

JANUARY 5

"And how did you find your steak?" inquired the manager of a famous restaurant from one of his better customers.

"I just moved the boiled potato," was the pointed reply, "and there it was."

JANUARY 6

Two young executives were competing for the favors of the shapely new secretary whose provocative dress caressed both their imaginations.

"She should be oriented on the differences between right and wrong," suggested the first budding genius.

"Great idea," joyfully echoed the second. "You teach her what's right and I'll teach her what's wrong."

JANUARY 7

To test a fortune telling machine whose accuracy had been highly advertised a young man inquired as to the current location of his father. Out came a card stating, "Your father is fishing in Canada."

The young man chortled with glee for he had just watched his mother and father depart on an overseas trip.

"My mother and father are on their way to Europe," he wrote and he dropped the information back into the machine.

Instantly there was a great deal of noise and lights lit up accompanied by whirring noises as the machine wrestled with this latest challenge to its ability and within moments out came another card on which was inscribed, "Your mother and her husband are on their way to Europe. Your father is still fishing in Canada."

JANUARY 8

While carving the chicken at a dinner party the surgeon accidentally let the fowl slip off the table and on to the lap of a nearby guest.

"Considering what has just happened I don't know if I would permit you to operate on me," the lady chided.

Pulling himself up to his full height and to his complete sense of retaliation the surgeon snapped, "You, madam, are no chicken."

JANUARY 9

The high school teacher was annoyed because someone had scribbled on the blackboard, "Johnny Green can kiss better than anybody else in the class."

Angrily she demanded to know the identity of the culprit but no one spoke.

"Very well," she finally shouted, "each and every one of you will be punished until we uncover the guilty one. Johnny Green, we'll start with you and keep you in after school."

The next morning the teacher was startled when she entered her classroom for on the board this time, in large letters, was written, "It pays to advertise."

JANUARY 10

A husband and wife sought help from a marriage counsellor.

"I don't know why we're having trouble," explained the husband. "We've been married twenty years and there's nothing she wouldn't do for me."

"That's the trouble," the counsellor pointed out. "You just won't do anything for each other."

JANUARY 11

A young man went into a department store and told the saleslady he was looking for a present for his girl friend.

"Would you like to see something nice in a dress?" asked the saleslady.

"Sure," was the eager reply, "but let's take care of the present first."

JANUARY 12

"Honey," said the prospective employer to the good looking girl applying for the secretary's job, "if I put my arms around you and kissed you, would you yell for help?"

"Would you need any?" she inquired drily.

JANUARY 13

A father took his four year old son to the zoo. When they came to the caged stork the little boy looked at it a long time before he finally exclaimed disappointedly, "Dad, he doesn't even recognize me!"

11

JANUARY 14

A hen and a pig were walking down the road when they spied a sign on a billboard that read, "Ham and eggs make the greatest breakfast in the world."

It made the hen proud.

"Terrific!" she boasted. "Doesn't it make you feel grand to realize we're making such an enormous contribution to humanity?"

The pig shook his head.

"It may be just a contribution to you," he observed soberly, "but to me it's an entire commitment."

JANUARY 15

A high school youngster kept failing history repeatedly. No matter how hard he tried he was never able to learn enough to pass any of the examinations. Finally, his mother, frustrated to the point of exasperation wrote a letter to the teacher in which she said, "If you wouldn't keep asking him about things that happened before he was even born maybe he would pass."

JANUARY 16

An old bull and a young bull were carefully eyeing four young cows standing at the far corner of the pasture.

"Let's run down and make love to one of them," urged the young bull.

"Let's just walk down," calmly suggested the older animal, "and make love to all of them."

JANUARY 17

At a seance a spiritualist told a widow that her recently deceased husband had been contacted in the next world.

"Is there anything he wants?" asked the enthusiastic widow. "Is there anything I can do to make him happy?"

After a few moments the spiritualist replied, "Yes, he says for you to send him a carton of cigarettes."

"I'll do it right away," was the cheerful response. "And just where shall I send them?"

"He doesn't give any address," noted the spiritualist, "but he also doesn't ask for any matches."

JANUARY 18

"I have a complaint to make," the annoyed lady told the superintendent of the apartment building where she lived. "Do you know who came to see me at three o'clock this morning?"

"No," was the reply. "Who?"

"No one," she announced disgustedly, "and that's my complaint."

JANUARY 19

In the name of efficiency a certain hospital assigned each of its nurses a number corresponding to a group of specified duties. Number one nurse had charge of the narcotics; number two nurse poured and distributed medicines, and so on.

Needing a nurse to change a patient's dressing one day a staff physician checked the nurses' bulletin board, found the right code number and went prospecting.

"Are you number four nurse?" he asked a pretty lady in white.

"I'm sorry," she smiled, "but you have the wrong number."

13

JANUARY 20

A retired bus driver anxious to keep himself occupied sat on his front porch day after day counting the buses and checking their schedules as they passed by. On Sunday, however, he totally ignored them.

Intrigued by such behavior one of his neighbors asked him for an explanation.

"Because," he answered tersely, "I don't want to work on my day off."

JANUARY 21

"Ninety-six cents a dozen for eggs?" shouted the irate housewife. "Scandalous! Why, that's eight cents an egg."

"I know," sympathized the grocer, "but remember, one egg represents a whole day's work for the hen."

JANUARY 22

The governor was very ill and the lieutenant governor visited him in the hospital.

Encased in an oxygen tent as he struggled for each breath of air the dying governor said, "I know I haven't treated you right and that I've kept you from advancing in the party but I hope, under the circumstances, that you can forgive me."

"Of course," the lieutenant governor assured him. "I'm not the sort who holds grudges and to prove it I'll do anything you ask."

"Then take your foot off the oxygen hose," gasped the governor.

JANUARY 23

They had a joint checking account but she beat him to the draw.

JANUARY 24

Al and Joe had been partners for years and they trusted each other implicitly. Came the day when Al took a much needed vacation. A few days later he got an emergency call from Joe.

"Ten thousand dollars is missing from our checking account," yelled Joe excitedly. "What shall I do?"

"Put it back," Al advised calmly.

JANUARY 25

Immediately after the wedding ceremony a newly married couple went to the photographer where they posed for a series of wedding pictures. A few weeks later the proofs arrived.

When they opened the envelopes, however, they saw a number of poses of a baby lying on a rug. Accompanying them was the following typewritten request.

"Please state clearly how many you want and what size."

JANUARY 26

An idiot got out of bed to answer the phone at 3:00 a.m. Unfortunately it was a wrong number and the voice at the other end apologized profusely for making such an error at so unearthly an hour.

"That's all right," minimized the idiot, "I had to get up anyhow to answer the phone."

JANUARY 27

An eligible bachelor and a prospective bride were brought together for their initial meeting by a most energetic and imaginative matchmaker. One look, though and the young man ran desperately for cover.

Drawing the matchmaker aside he whispered, "What did you get me into! This is terrible! You said she was a beauty but instead she's fat, ugly, has a glass eye and a wooden leg."

"You can talk louder," the matchmaker assured him. "She's deaf too."

JANUARY 28

When oil was discovered on his land the uneducated farmer became an instant millionaire. Unable to write his name he had always had an agreement with the bank that permitted him to sign his name with two crosses.

He continued the practice and all went well for several months when the bank began receiving his checks with three cross marks on them instead of the usual two and they immediately contacted him for verification.

"They're my checks all right," he assured them.

"But why the three crosses?" asked one of the bank officials.

"It's my wife's idea," explained the rustic. "She thinks I'm rich enough now to have a middle name."

JANUARY 29

If you marry for money you'll earn it.

JANUARY 30

"How much are those giant sized candy bars?" inquired a youngster of the storekeeper.

"Two for a quarter," was the reply.

"And how much is one of them?"

"Fifteen cents."

"Then give me the other one," said the lad.

A group of doctors who met regularly for lunch were saddened by the death of Sam, their favorite waiter, who had looked after them for years. When one of them heard he could possibly be contacted in the Great Beyond he talked the others into attending a seance even though some of them didn't consider it scientific.

They all sat quietly around a large table with the lights dulled as the medium went to work.

"Sam," she said, "are you there?"

No response.

"Sam," she urged again, "can you hear me?"

Still no response.

She tried repeatedly but each time she struck out and her pleas went for nought.

Yet she refused to give up for she was sure she could make contact with the departed waiter.

"Sam," she said, "why don't you answer. I know you hear me, I can feel it. Please, Sam, talk."

Again she was greeted with the same deadly silence.

Finally, in desperation, she demanded, "Why don't you answer me?"

At which an irate voice snapped, "That's not my table!"

LETTER OF THE MONTH

Everyone with a problem welcomes advice and will always listen to what he hears even though he may not accept the counsel that's offered.

It's been like that all through the ages but our ancestors lacked the outlets we have and "advice" columns as such were not available to them despite their being as eager for help as we are.

It is not too late. Imagination being what it is, we can roll back the calendar and provide them with the catharsis they lacked during their lifetimes. In other words, if the Muse of history could have been the chief dispenser of instant wisdom it all might have sounded something like what is reported below.

Macedonia

Dear Miss History:

My record is perfect. I have never lost a battle. From my native Macedonia to India my armies have conquered every nation along the way. I am invincible!

But I am also bored! Utterly! With no more worlds left to conquer what can I do to remain active?

Alexander the Great

Dear Al:

Try the seven year itch.

LIFE'S LITTLE PHILOSOPHIES

Confidence
  is
    buying
      a
        bottle
          of
            hair
              restorer
                from
                a
                  bald
                    headed
                      salesman.

Love
  is
    a
      little
        itch
          on the
            heart
              that
                you
                  can't
                    scratch.

FEBRUARY 1

This one is being presented with apologies to Goldilocks.

Three polar bears were seated on an iceberg.
"I've got a tale to tell," announced Papa Bear.
Said Mama Bear, "I too have a tale to tell."
Chirped the Baby Bear, "My tale's told."

FEBRUARY 2

Realizing that he would one day have to face the inevitable a wealthy man consulted his lawyer.

"I'm a compulsive character," he confided, "and I want things done a certain way. When I go I want you to find me the most expensive automobile available. I want you to have me dressed up in sport clothes, put me at the wheel of the car, and lower me into my permanent home just like that."

"But it will cost you a lot of money," protested the attorney. "Do you have any idea how much land it will take to accommodate you like that?"

"I have enough money to cover everything and also to give you a handsome fee for your trouble," was the reply. "Just do it."

The lawyer finally agreed and when the time came he

carried out the program exactly as planned. It was a memorable sight and as the car with the deceased at the wheel was being guided into the grave one of the mourners, impressed by the proceedings, turned to someone at his side and remarked admiringly, "Man, that's living!"

FEBRUARY 3

"And how would you like your hair cut?" the barber inquired of the five year old tyke.

"Like my daddy's," was the innocent answer. "With a hole on top."

FEBRUARY 4

"Doctor," asked the young man nervously, "If I don't drink, smoke or go out with girls will I live to be a hundred?"

"No," was the responding quip, "but it will sure seem like it."

FEBRUARY 5

"Great city, Paris," said Tom to his friend on his return from a trip abroad. "Wish I had gone there twenty-five years ago."

"When Paris was Paris?" inquired the friend.

"No," was the wistful reply. "When Tom was Tom."

FEBRUARY 6

"Why did you go over my head?" the employer demanded of the timid clerk.

"Not me," stuttered the milquetoast. "I'd never do anything like that."

"Then how come I heard you praying for a raise?" shouted the boss.

FEBRUARY 7

"You better listen to this very carefully," a lady warned her friend. "I can only tell it once because I promised faithfully never to repeat it."

FEBRUARY 8

A middle-aged raconteur told his friend, "I had a wonderful dream last night. I was at the beach, the sun was shining, the water was just right, and I spent the whole day there."

Said his friend, "I had a dream too. I ran across two beautiful girls and we went to a motel room and had a ball."

The first man was envious. "If you had two girls why didn't you get in touch with me?" he demanded.

"I did," replied the friend, "but your wife told me you had gone to the beach."

FEBRUARY 9

Two soldiers were sweating it out in a foxhole during a particularly heavy barrage. One of them constantly moved around in an effort to reach a safe spot. His frantic motions were in direct contrast to another soldier who was seated quietly in a corner. Finally the calm one spoke up.

"Relax," he advised his jittery companion. "No use worrying or running around. In this war every bullet has a name on it and if there's one with your monicker it will find you no matter where you hide."

"I'm not afraid of the ones with names on," was the cautious reply. "I'm just scared of the ones that say, 'To whom it may concern.'"

FEBRUARY 10

"If you really loved me," a wife needled her husband, "you would have married someone else."

FEBRUARY 11

"Take a glass of whiskey at regular intervals," a doctor advised the patient who had complained of insomnia.

"And will that put me to sleep?" inquired the patient hopefully.

"No," answered the physician, "but it will make you satisfied to stay awake."

FEBRUARY 12

The henpecked husband weighed himself on a scale that issued a card with the poundage on one side and the individual's fortune on the flip side.

With wonderful enjoyment he read, "You are brave, strong, decisive, and courageous. Success is within your grasp."

Looking over his shoulder his wife, who had witnessed it all, snorted, "And they didn't get your weight right, either."

FEBRUARY 13

"What are you here for?" the judge asked the first boy.

"Throwing peanuts in the water, sir," was the reply.

"And you?" the judge asked the second boy.

"Throwing peanuts in the water, sir," was the same answer.

"And I suppose you threw peanuts in the water, too?" said the jurist to the third boy.

"No, sir," was the reply. "I'm Peanuts."

FEBRUARY 14

"Here comes old icy fingers," one cow said to another as the farmer approached on a cold morning.

FEBRUARY 15

"How long have you been working at the plant?" one man inquired of another.

"Ever since they threatened to fire me," was the retort.

FEBRUARY 16

Needing information for his homework a little boy asked his mother, "How was I born?"

Convinced that he had not yet reached the age of understanding the parent replied, "The stork brought you, darling."

"And how was Daddy born?" followed up the youngster.

"The same way," said his mother.

"And Grandma?"

"The stork brought her too."

"And what about Grandpa?"

"Same way. No change."

Whereupon the little fellow sighed and wrote, "According to the most reliable sources there have been no natural births in our family for the last three generations."

FEBRUARY 17

The newlyweds were having their first argument.

"I want you to know that more than a dozen men proposed to me," the wife bragged.

"Then why didn't you marry the first fool that came along?" demanded the husband.

"I did," she replied.

FEBRUARY 18

A seven year old girl came home one afternoon and complained loudly to her mother that a little boy had kissed her at school.

"And just how did he do that?" inquired her mother.

"It wasn't easy," cried the girl. "It took three other girls to help me catch him."

FEBRUARY 19

A dignified old gentleman decided to destroy his pet male parrot because of the bird's constant cussing.

"I'm broadminded as a rule," he explained to a friend, "but his vocabulary is so appalling that I simply can't stand it. He's got to go."

"Not so fast," cautioned the friend. "I've got a parrot too and she's the exact opposite. Not a wrong word comes out of her mouth and most of the time she's involved in prayer. I never saw such a saintly bird. Why not try an experiment and put the two parrots together. Maybe mine will cure yours of his faults. It's worth a try, isn't it?"

"I guess so," conceded the old gentleman.

The next day he brought over his parrot and put him in the cage with the other bird. The male parrot, unquestionably pleased with his new location, chirped to his suddenly acquired cagemate, "Hi, babe, how about some fun."

A smile crossed the lady parrot's face as she chuckled, "At last my prayers have been answered."

FEBRUARY 20

She was at that awkward age when her voice was changing from no to yes.

FEBRUARY 21

"Do you have a steady girl friend?" the young man was asked.

"No, sir," was the deferential reply, "and I don't have an unsteady one either."

FEBRUARY 22

"My husband thinks he's a horse," a woman complained. "Can you possibly cure him?"

"Yes," the psychiatrist assured her, "but it will take a great deal of money."

"No problem," she commented cheerfully. "He just won the Derby."

FEBRUARY 23

During the early days of the Old West a poker game was in progress in one of the saloons when the dealer suddenly jumped up, drew his gun, and shouted, "This game is crooked! Bronco Buster over there ain't playing the hand I dealt him."

FEBRUARY 24

A father strongly objected to his daughter's latest boy friend. Several times he tried to break them up but to no avail. It seemed the harder he tried the more his daughter resisted him.

One night when both youngsters were in the living room with the lights out he decided his patience had been exhausted. Barging in he flipped the lights on and shouted, "I'll teach you to make love to my daughter."

"I wish you would," encouraged the youth, "because I'm sure not doing any good on my own."

FEBRUARY 25

"What are you in for?" a jailbird inquired of his new cellmate.

"Borrowing money," was the seemingly innocent reply.

"But they don't put you in jail for that," the old timer pointed out.

"Well," drawled the newcomer, "the guy I borrowed it from was a little stubborn and I had to hit him over the head before he lent it to me."

FEBRUARY 26

In the middle of the night a wife was suddenly wakened by her husband's talking in his sleep.

"It's in the phone book," he shouted frantically as his loud voice pierced every corner of the room. "It's in the phone book."

It frightened her and she woke him at once.

"What's the trouble?" she pleaded, deeply concerned.

"I was dreaming," he explained, "that the income tax people wanted to pay me a refund but they couldn't do it because they couldn't find my address."

FEBRUARY 27

She had a wonderfully magnetic personality. Everything on her was charged.

FEBRUARY 28

Al and Sam had been good friends over the years even though the former had become a great success and the latter was just an average plodder.

One day Sam got a long distance call from Florida.

"Sam," said the voice, "guess what? It's me. Al. And

guess what else? I'm calling you from a telephone in my own car. Isn't that wonderful?"

"A telephone?" gasped Sam. "In your own car?"

"Yes," confirmed Al. "A telephone! In my own car!"

Sam was crushed because his friend's affluence had finally overawed him. Right then and there he vowed he would catch up with Al regardless of what he would have to do to accomplish it.

First he withdrew all the money from his savings account. Then, in rapid succession, he mortgaged his home, floated a loan on his business, and pawned some of his most cherished private possessions. Finally, he accumulated enough funds to buy a car with a telephone in it. Then he gleefully sat back and put in a call to Al's car in Miami.

"This is Sam," he shouted to his friend when Al answered. "I'm calling you from the telephone in my car here in New York."

"Sorry I can't hear you," Al shouted back. "My other phone's ringing."

LETTER OF THE MONTH

Athens

Dear Miss History:

To impress our citizens with the urgent need to think I repeatedly stopped them in the public square and asked them important questions that made them use their minds. They didn't like it and decided I was provoking them too much. They had me brought to trial and I was convicted for being a corrupter and a disbeliever.

It's all terribly unfair! I tried to be a public spirited citizen and to improve the quality of our lives but instead of rewarding me the court sentenced me to death and ordered me to drink the fatal hemlock.

Please, Miss History, what can I do?

Socrates

Dear Soc:

Eat first! Never drink on an empty stomach.

AND ONE FOR LEAP YEAR

Asia Minor

Dear Miss History:

Although I am the richest man in the world I am also

frustrated because I can't buy the one thing I want most—happiness.

Can you help me? Please?

Croesus

Dear Moneybags:

You've been shopping in the wrong places.

LIFE'S LITTLE PHILOSOPHIES

An
  optimist
    is
      a
        pregnant
          teenager
            rubbing
              her
                abdomen
                  with
                    vanishing
                    cream.

Women
  who
    live
      in
        glass
          houses
            should
              wear
                stylish
                  lingerie.

31

MARCH 1

A man with laryngitis went into a drug store for medicine for his throat. The only person behind the counter at the moment was a beautiful young blonde.

"Is the pharmacist in?" he managed to whisper to her.

"No," she whispered in reply. "Come on into the back."

MARCH 2

The taciturn young man was taking his best girl friend for a drive along a picturesque country road. It was Sunday afternoon, all was quiet and peaceful, the young lady was very pretty and the entire setting so inspired him that he suddenly blurted out, "Will you marry me?"

The girl, although surprised, was alert enough to recognize her opportunity and she quickly replied, "Sure will."

There was a thorough silence after that and it continued for another hour. The young lady was afraid to break it for she did not want to offend her prospective husband in any way. Finally, however, she couldn't hold out any longer and she carefully inquired, "Don't you want to talk?"

"I already talked too much," was the snappy comeback.

MARCH 3

Sign in an undertaker's window.
"Pay Now. Go Later."

MARCH 4

The man seemed confused. He had entered the department store and slowly approached one of the counters in the ladies clothing department and then stopped suddenly as if unaware of what to do next. On noticing his dilemma a solicitous clerk approached him and asked, "Can I help you?"

"I hope so," he sighed. "I was supposed to get a camisole or a casserole but I can't remember which."

"No trouble," responded the clerk with a touch of deviltry in her voice. "Just tell me what kind of a chicken you want to put into it."

MARCH 5

Two cars crashed into each other with a loud bang.
"What's the matter?" roared one of the drivers. "You blind?"
"Blind?" retorted the other. "I hit you, didn't I?"

MARCH 6

After a wealthy man's demise there was a great deal of interest in the bequests he had made. When the will was probated one of his old friends asked the lawyer involved, "Did the deceased leave his wife a lot?"

"Every chance he got," was the sage reply.

MARCH 7

The patient had a marked inferiority complex and he was seeking much needed help from his psychiatrist. To encourage him the doctor urged, "Build up your self-image. Keep telling yourself that you're a worthwhile human being, that you've got ability, that you're a somebody. Keep that up and you're bound to be successful."

The patient, however, shook his head sadly.

"No use," he lamented. "I know only too well what a big liar I am."

MARCH 8

The customer in the restaurant was unusually glum when he gave the waitress his order.

"I want two pieces of burned toast," he said, "some cold coffee that tastes like mud and a pair of overdone fried eggs that stretch like rubber."

Accustomed to odd requests the waitress did exactly as she was bid. She soon returned with toast that was charred, coffee that was thick and tasteless as well as cold and a pair of eggs that could have bounced off the floor if they were dropped.

"Anything else, sir?" she inquired dutifully.

"Yes," directed the customer. "Sit down and nag me. I want to make believe I'm back home."

MARCH 9

A bartender was astounded when a gorilla came in, plunked his frame on a stool and calmly ordered a martini. Not wanting to create any disturbance the bartender dutifully served him.

"That will be five dollars, please," he told the beast.

The gorilla paid and started to sip his drink. The bartender maintained his silence for a while but an overpowering curiosity finally forced him to speak. Approaching the gorilla cautiously he said, "This is the first time I've ever served someone like yourself."

"And at five dollars a drink it's sure going to be the last time," retorted the gorilla.

MARCH 10

At her wedding breakfast the oft married bride spilled some food on her gown.

"Oh, dear," she moaned, "and this is only the first time I've worn it."

MARCH 11

"I'm one of you," the city-bred politician insisted when he addressed a rural audience. "I can milk cows, slop the hogs, and plough as straight a furrow as any man. Why, there isn't a thing on a farm that I can't do."

"Lay an egg!" challenged a heckler.

MARCH 12

"What do you do at the office that takes you a whole day?" a young tyke inquired of his father.

"Nothing," replied the parent honestly.

"Then how do you know when you're finished," asked the lad.

MARCH 13

The wife was beside herself.

"How can you say such beastly things to me," she cried to her husband. "And after I've given you the best years of my life."

Amazed, he retorted, "You mean those were the best years?"

MARCH 14

Two morons were out hunting and when a rabbit scooted by, one of them quickly took aim.

"Hey!" shouted the other. "You can't shoot. Your gun's not loaded."

"Can't stop to load it now," was the hurried reply. "That rabbit just won't wait."

MARCH 15

The young man approached the social worker rather brashly.

"Do you save wayward girls?" he asked.

"Absolutely," she confirmed.

"Then save me a couple for next Saturday night," he shot back.

MARCH 16

"Can you tell me how long cows should be milked?" inquired the city dude.

"Same as short cows," quipped the farmer.

MARCH 17

"Once upon a time," related a local big wig trying to impress his audience with his own ability to overcome adversity, "things were very tough for me. I remember one day especially. I had been out of work for months and I was behind in my rent. I owed so much on my furniture that they were getting ready to repossess it. My children had no decent clothing to wear. The future looked dark and hopeless. As a matter of fact it was all so bad and I was so depressed that I sat down in front of the house and tried to figure a way out of my troubles.

"A well meaning neighbor came over, patted me on the

back and said, 'Cheer up. Things can always get worse.'

"So I cheered up and, sure enough, things got worse."

MARCH 18

"Where did you get that black eye?"

"Her husband," was the sad answer.

"But I thought he was out of town."

"So did I."

MARCH 19

"If you've been treating me for a split personality," a patient inquired of his psychiatrist, "how come I have to pay the whole bill?"

MARCH 20

A politician running for sheriff decided to contact everyone in the county during his campaign. All went well until he got to the rural areas where distances became an important factor. At the end of one particular day he was so far from his headquarters and his home that he decided it would be wiser to put up somewhere close for the night rather than travel to and from his base. Accordingly when he stopped at the next farmhouse he investigated the possibilities of overnight accommodations.

A very beautiful lady came to the door and when the politician explained his problem to her she gladly offered to help him.

"I want you to know that you're very welcome to spend the night here," she said, "but I also think you ought to know that I'm a widow and I live here alone."

The politician thought it over very carefully and finally he said, "I certainly want to thank you for your kind offer and frankly, I'm flattered. Under ordinary circumstances

I would be delighted to avail myself of your wonderful invitation but, since I'm running for sheriff, I have to be very careful. If word of this ever leaked out I'd be in serious trouble and I could easily lose the election. If you don't mind, though, I'd like to bed down in your barn if that's all right with you."

The widow was both surprised and disappointed but she consented.

"I'll be gone by early morning," the politician promised, "and I won't be the least bother to you."

All went well and he had a restful night considering the conditions but he was awakened early the next morning by some rather strange sounds in the barn. Looking up he spied the widow poking a bull rather vigorously in an attempt to mate him with a nearby cow. The bull, however, kept resisting despite the widow's efforts and finally, in desperation, she shouted at the animal, "What's the matter. You running for sheriff too?"

MARCH 21

Appearing late for a dinner party the lady excused herself with the alibi, "Sorry but I was held up at the beauty parlor."

Snapped back the deeply annoyed hostess, "Too bad they didn't have time to wait on you."

MARCH 22

Said one flea to the other when they came out of the movie, "Do we walk or take a dog?"

MARCH 23

Sign in a store window read, "Why go somewhere else to get cheated when you can come here?"

MARCH 24

"I don't stand for necking," the girl announced firmly on her first date with a young man.

"You don't?" asked her surprised escort.

"No," she said, "standing makes me tired."

MARCH 25

"How far is it to the nearest gas station?" asked the stranded motorist.

"Two miles as the crow flies," replied the farmer.

"And just how far would it be," snapped the exasperated motorist, "if that crow had to walk and roll a flat tire at the same time?"

MARCH 26

The lawyer carefully explained to his client that he could not afford a divorce.

"It's too expensive," said the attorney. "You haven't got that kind of money. The best thing for you to do is forget it."

The client was obviously disappointed.

"And what," he demanded, "is the next best thing?"

MARCH 27

"If a fellow took you to a show one night," a girl asked her friend, "dinner the following night, and a concert the third night and never tried to kiss you on any of those dates what exactly would you do?"

"Lie about it," was the instant retort.

MARCH 28

A man struck it rich when he found a bag in the street with one hundred thousand dollars in it. The news immediately made the front pages and in one of the interviews that followed he was asked if he would return the money if someone claimed it.

"Of course," he replied anxious to demonstrate his basic sense of generosity but then he hurriedly added, "that is, if the owner is a poor man."

MARCH 29

To reinforce his request for a raise an employee confided to his boss that three companies were after him.

"Three?" shouted the angry employer. "And just who are they?"

"The gas, electric, and telephone companies," was the careful reply.

MARCH 30

"Do you think I'll look good in tails?" a man asked his sarcastic wife.

"Why not!" she retorted. "Your ancestors did!"

MARCH 31

A young man had been calling on a girl every night for five years. Finally he was asked if he was ever going to marry her. That practically shocked him.

"Marry her?" he recoiled as if struck by a sharp blow. "If I did that just where would I spend my evenings?"

LETTER OF THE MONTH

Paris, France

Dear Miss History:

Even though I am the king's favorite and my every wish is immediately granted I am worried.

A fortune teller here at court recently predicted that there will be an Industrial Revolution during which machines will replace humans.

If that is true what will happen to people like me who are not trained for anything special?

Jeanne du Barry

Dear Jeannie:

No machine can ever replace what you have to offer.

LIFE'S LITTLE PHILOSOPHIES

Advice
   is
     like
       medicine.
         Easy
           to
             give
               but
                 hard
                   to
                     take.

When
   you're
     down
       in
         the
           mouth
             always
               remember
                 that
                   JONAH
                     still
                       came
                         out
                           all
                             right.

APRIL 1

When twilight comes, I sit alone
And dream of the days with Mabel,
Slowly there comes a tear to my eye,
There's an onion on the table.

APRIL 2

He was so ill his doctor advised him not to read any continued stories.

APRIL 3

A father caught his son making love to one of the neighborhood girls.

Annoyed, the parent demanded, "Don't you have anything better to do?"

"Like what, Dad?" asked the son.

"Like studying," suggested the father.

"Studying isn't better than this," observed the youngster.

APRIL 4

A patient, hospitalized for the removal of his thyroid gland, woke up in the recovery room after surgery and found a bandage around his abdomen as well as one around his neck.

"Why is that?" he inquired of his surgeon.

"A lot of other doctors were watching me in the operating room," explained the medic, "and they liked my work so well that I took out your appendix as an encore."

APRIL 5

Aware of the requirements of his eventual exit a certain gentleman inspected several cemeteries and eventually came to one that was unusually pretentious and expensive. Obviously only the wealthy could afford it. The mausoleums were large and imposing, the art work in them was flawless, and the surrounding landscape was remarkably eye-catching.

He was so deeply impressed that when he arrived home that evening he described what he had seen to his wife in the most laudatory terms.

"What a cemetery!" he enthused. "And you should see how stylishly the rich people live there."

APRIL 6

A wealthy citizen gave the taxi driver only a twenty-five cent tip when his bill was over five dollars.

The disappointed cabbie protested.

"I drive your daughter around a lot," he said, "and she always gives me a much bigger tip than that."

Retorted the richman, "My daughter has a wealthy father. I haven't."

APRIL 7

A patient needed a tooth extracted and was told by his dentist that the cost would be fifty dollars.

"Fifty dollars?" yelped the victim. "To take out a tooth?"

"That's my fee," the dentist quietly said.

"And just how long will the job take?"

"No more than a few minutes," the dentist assured him.

"Not on your life," was the objection. "I absolutely refuse to pay prices like that."

"I can pull it out slowly if it will make you feel better," offered the dentist.

APRIL 8

Persistence has always been classified as a virtue. Which brings to mind the yarn about the debonair young man who invariably dated school teachers.

One day he was asked to explain his behavior and he replied, "A school teacher will always insist that if you don't do it right the first time you keep doing it over and over until you do get it right."

Case closed.

APRIL 9

A moron was having difficulty walking with a cane because it was too tall for him.

"Why don't you cut a few inches off the bottom," a friend suggested.

"What for," argued the moron. "It's the upper end that's too high."

APRIL 10

"Hi, Ben," greeted a friend. "Haven't seen you in years. Still working for the same outfit?"

"Yep," was the curt response. "Same wife and five kids."

APRIL 11

A man had recently been involved in a serious accident and his head was still swathed in bandages, his leg was in a cast and he had to hobble around on crutches.

"What happened?" inquired a much concerned friend.

"I was driving along Main Street," he explained, "minding my own business and paying strict attention to all the traffic rules when a woman driving the car ahead of me signalled for a right turn."

"And?" prompted the friend.

"And she made a right turn," was the sad reply.

APRIL 12

After her husband passed on the widow managed to contact him in the next world through a medium.

"Are you happy?" she asked.

"Very," replied the departed.

"Happier than you were with me on earth?"

"Much happier."

"Tell me," she encouraged, "what's Heaven like."

"Heaven?" was the astonished comeback. "Who's in Heaven!"

APRIL 13

Plugging his new elixir the spieler at the sideshow yelled, "This will give you new life, ladies and gentlemen.

Unconditionally guaranteed! This little bottle of miraculous liquid will keep you forever young. It cannot fail because it has the secret of eternal youth in it. If you want proof look at me. Take a close look because whether you believe it or not, I am over two hundred years old."

"Is that really true?" someone asked of the spieler's assistant.

"Can't say," answered the helper. "I've only been with him a hundred and twenty five years myself."

APRIL 14

At a recent premiere of a well-known movie a man and his dog sat in the audience, completely enthralled by what they saw. Especially the dog. With each heart rending scene he sobbed aloud and it was obvious that he was undergoing a tremendous emotional experience.

When the performance was over and the audience was leaving the theater the manager approached the canine's owner.

"Your dog sure enjoyed the show," he observed.

"He sure did," agreed the owner, "but the funny thing is he didn't care much for the book."

APRIL 15

A fighter was being mauled from one end of the ring to the other and when he returned to his corner at the end of the round his manager decided that a psychological uplift was unquestionably needed.

"You're doing great, kid," he encouraged. "That bum hasn't laid a glove on you."

The battered pugilist, however, was not fooled. Squinting through his badly swollen eyes he said, "Then you better keep watching the referee because somebody in that ring is knocking the devil out of me."

47

APRIL 16

When the undertaker asked him if he wanted his mother-in-law's remains cremated, embalmed, or buried, the much harassed son-in-law instantly shot back, "Take no chances! Do all three!"

APRIL 17

Two men were ogling a pair of curvaceous lovelies in bathing suits doing their sitting up exercises on the beach. The ladies went through their routines with vigor and grace and it was obvious that the two gentlemen were enjoying the performance immensely.

"Terrific," applauded one of the men, "but do you really think it's good for reducing?"

"Absolutely," confirmed the other gentleman. "I walk five miles every day just to watch them."

APRIL 18

"You look terrible," one friend told the other. "What's happened to you?"

"No sleep last night," was the reply.

"How come?"

"Well it was like this. When I went up to my hotel after midnight I found an exquisite blonde in a fetching negligee stretched out on my couch. I had no idea who she was or why she was there so, considering the circumstances, I closed the door quietly and went down to the lobby where I tried to get some shut eye in one of their chairs. Wouldn't you be tired after a night like that?"

"Sure," was the reply, "but I don't think you ought to lie about it."

APRIL 19

Having just been taken on a guided tour through an acquaintance's new apartment the guest thought it only appropriate to make some flattering comments. Accordingly she said, "You have a lovely place here and period furniture too. Remarkable."

"Yes," said the hostess, "half of it goes back to Louis the Fourteenth."

"And the other half?" inquired the guest.

"It goes back to the finance company on the first."

APRIL 20

On observing his fiftieth wedding anniversary a husband was asked to explain the secret of his lengthy and successful marriage.

"No secret," he replied. "We decided a long time ago to share things right down the middle of the line and do it all on a fifty fifty basis. Equality! That was our watchword. That's why half the time my wife made the decisions and the other half of the time I took her suggestions."

APRIL 21

"Will I be able to read after you give me the new glasses?" the patient asked his ophthalmologist.

"Of course," confirmed the specialist.

"Wonderful," bubbled the patient, "considering I've never learned how to read."

APRIL 22

The photographer was taking a picture of a father and his son.

"Have your boy put his arm around you," he told the

parent. "That will make it all look more natural."

"If you're looking for something natural," cracked the father, "I'll have the boy put his hand in my pocket."

APRIL 23

The little tyke was a guest at a wedding. When the proceedings were over he was confused and he said to his mother, "Did the bride change her mind?"

"No," was the answer. "Why?"

"Because," said the youngster, "she went down the aisle with one man and came back with another."

APRIL 24

Late in November little Jimmy's Daddy asked him what he wanted for Christmas from Santa Claus.

"Please," requested the boy, "can I have a baby brother?"

The father hesitated for he realized that such a question required a tactful reply.

Finally he explained, "Santa is pretty busy so near Christmas and I don't think he could do it on such short notice."

Whereupon Jimmy looked up hopefully as he inquired, "But couldn't he put a couple of extra men on the job?"

APRIL 25

The not so smart young lady was interviewed for a job and at the end her prospective employer asked, "Where can I get hold of you?"

"I don't know," she replied. "I'm awfully ticklish."

APRIL 26

A young lady employed by a greeting card company was fired when she mixed up the cards for expectant mothers with those that read, "Sorry about your recent accident."

APRIL 27

Ashamed to tell his wife that his doctor had diagnosed his malady as chronic alcoholism the patient searched his brain frantically for some sort of cover up story to tell his wife. On the way home he passed a music store that had a prominent display in the window featured by the word "Syncopation" in large letters. It caught his eye and as he scanned it an idea took shape in his mind and soon blossomed into a fully developed yarn. By the time he arrived home he was ready with his answers.

"What did the doctor find?" inquired his anxious wife.

"Something called 'Syncopation,'" he triumphantly replied.

"What's that?" asked the missus.

"Search me," said the patient. "You know these doctors. They never tell you anything."

His wife, however, refused to stop there. Bringing out the family dictionary she hunted up the word, "Syncopation" and found it most accurately defined as an uneven movement from bar to bar.

APRIL 28

"You're not handling your wife right," the bachelor told his married friend.

"What do you know about it," challenged the wedded one. "You're not even married."

"I'm no egg either," retorted the bachelor, "but I sure can tell a good egg from a bad one."

APRIL 29

Irate voice over the telephone, "Okay, stupid, if this is the wrong number why did you answer the phone."

APRIL 30

"Do you have notions?" the lady customer inquired of the department store clerk.

"Sure do," he cheerfully admitted, "but not during working hours."

LETTER OF THE MONTH

Outside Eden

Dear Miss History:

I am sure you know that I am well along in years, very well along. I hold the record for longevity, a record that may never be broken.

During my long life I have, of course, had numerous experiences with the fair sex and, as a result, I find that women are no longer a mystery to me. I have learned to recognize all their whims and their fancies and I can read them like a book.

What do you think of that!

Methuselah

Dear Father Time:

Maybe you can read women like a book but at your age you are certainly too old to start a library.

LIFE'S LITTLE PHILOSOPHIES

People
who
scratch
themselves
in
public
are
the
only
ones
who
know
where
it
itches.

Marriage
is
the
biggest
cause
of
divorce.

MAY 1

"Ladies Ready To Wear Clothes" announced the sign over the entrance to the new store catering exclusively to women's apparel.

"About time," growled the old villager as he read it.

MAY 2

A man walked into a lawyer's office and pointed a gun at him.

"What's wrong?" pleaded the attorney.

"Your rotten advice is what's wrong," was the acid reply. "Twenty years ago I wanted to kill my wife but you talked me out of it by warning me I'd get twenty years in the penitentiary if I did it. And like a fool I listened to you."

"That was the right thing to do," the lawyer assured him.

"In the pig's neck it was," snapped the man. "If I had done what I wanted to do I'd be a free man today."

MAY 3

An efficiency expert had passed on and his coffin was being borne to its final resting place by six dignified pall bearers. Suddenly the lid flew open and he sat up and shouted to the undertaker, "If you put this thing on wheels you can lay off four men."

MAY 4

The society matron was giving her new maid final instructions for the party she was having that night. "I want you to stand at the door and call the guests' names as they come in," she directed.

"I sure will," the maid happily agreed. "I've been dying to call those kind of people names for years."

MAY 5

"I always take my wife wherever I go," admitted a husband. "It's better than kissing her goodbye."

MAY 6

Two ladies, playing golf very slowly, were annoying a couple of gentlemen behind them who were in a hurry to finish their game.

Finally, one of the gents, unable to endure it any longer, decided to take action and inform the ladies they intended to play through. As he approached them, however, he suddenly stopped and then hurriedly retraced his steps.

"What's the matter?" inquired his partner.

"Those two women up ahead," he announced excitedly. "Well, one of them is my wife and the other one is my mistress."

"In that case," offered his partner, "I'll go and talk to them."

In a few more moments, though, he too was back and equally red-faced.

"Small world, isn't it," was all he managed to utter.

MAY 7

After careful examination the doctor shook his head and told Mr. Jones, "I'm sorry but I'm afraid your wife's mind is gone."

The husband was not surprised.

"No wonder," he mused. "She's been giving me a piece of it every day for years."

MAY 8

On the first pay day after the honeymoon the dutiful husband gave his wife his entire pay check except for thirty dollars he held out for incidental expenses. The little woman was unquestionably satisfied.

On the next pay day, however, she was flabbergasted when he reversed the process and gave her only thirty dollars keeping the remainder of it for himself.

"But, darling," she pointed out patiently, "how do you expect me to take care of things on only thirty dollars."

"Darned if I know," was the retort, "but I had to do it last week and now it's your turn."

MAY 9

At the dawn of creation the Lord called everyone together and apportioned various favors. One of these was an active sex life and to Adam he said, "I give you twenty years."

Next he offered the same amount to the parrot but the bird graciously declined and explained, "I only need ten, Lord."

Remarkably alert Adam offered to take the other ten and since there were no objections the Lord granted Adam that favor.

Then the Lord also offered twenty years to the monkey.

"Thank you, Lord," said the monkey, "but all I really need is ten."

Again Adam offered to take the other ten even more gladly than before and again the Lord generously awarded them to him.

That's why today a man has twenty years of active sex life, ten years of monkeying around and ten years of talking about it.

MAY 10

To make a sure sale tell a woman you have something her neighbors say she can't afford.

MAY 11

Once upon a time there were three sisters who lived in a small town. Their names were Faith, Hope, and Charity.

Their lives were routine and monotonous and one day Faith, the oldest, decided to cut all local ties and seek her fortune in the big city.

She was gone a full year and when she returned for a short visit she was beautifully clothed, rode in a chauffeur driven limousine and it was obvious that she had been very successful.

Her prosperity prompted Hope, her younger sister to return to the big city with her.

Another year passed and this time it was Hope who returned for a visit. Just like Faith before her she too was togged out in expensive clothes and oozed with riches. The local people eyed her with envy and after a brief stay she returned to the city.

The following year both Faith and Hope came back to their home town together for their annual visit. This time they were met by their youngest sister who was exquisitely garbed and sported the most stylish furs. She rode in an expensive foreign car replete with both chauffeur and footman. Her success was dazzling and she had obviously outdistanced both her sisters.

After all the initial greetings had been exchanged and the superlative comments registered the youngest sister purred, "Don't be so surprised, girls. Remember, Charity begins at home."

MAY 12

"My ancestors didn't come over on the *MAY-FLOWER*," a society matron bragged with unmistakable snobbery. "They had a boat of their own."

MAY 13

A city man accustomed to urban problems was on a visit to a rural area. Eager to learn about rustic behavior he inquired of a farmer, "Are your neighbors honest?"

"Absolutely," was the confident reply.

"Then why do you keep that loaded gun near the chicken coop?" asked the visitor.

"That," explained the farmer, "is what keeps them honest."

MAY 14

"How many kegs of beer do you sell in a week?" a customer asked the bartender.

"About fifteen," was the reply.

"Want to sell thirty?"

"Of course," replied the eager bartender. "How?"

"Fill the glasses," was the pointed advice.

MAY 15

A total stranger walked into a physician's office and said, "Doctor, I want to thank you very much because I benefitted a great deal from your treatment."

"But you're not my patient," observed the surprised medic.

"True," agreed the stranger, "but my uncle was and I'm his heir."

MAY 16

There are some parents who try to impart distinctive names to their offsprings and in occasional instances the results have been mirthsome, to say the least, as in the following.

One youngster, saddled with a given name of Mergenthorpe, was playing with his buddies in the street when his mother stretched out of their apartment window and shouted down, "Mergenthorpe, darling, your lunch is ready. Come upstairs."

Mergenthorpe, though, was in the midst of a hectic ball game and he ignored the summons.

"Mergenthorpe," shouted his mother a second time. "Lunch is on the table. It's getting cold!"

Still there was no response.

"Mergenthorpe!" she literally screamed. "Come right up this instant!"

Whereupon one of the other youngsters playing with Mergenthorpe poked the lad in the ribs and said, "Hey, Stinkie, your mother's calling you."

MAY 17

A psychiatrist ran down the street with a couch strapped to his back.

"House call," he explained to a passing friend.

MAY 18

Three old men were sitting on a park bench as a beautiful and well-proportioned cutie walked by.

"If I were younger," asserted the first man, "I'd run after her and hug her."

"I'd not only hug her," insisted the second octagenarian, "but I'd kiss her too."

Somewhat confused the third oldster scratched his head as he remarked sadly, "Wasn't there something else we used to do?"

MAY 19

"Today we have everything on the menu, sir," the waitress announced proudly.

"So I see," noted the customer drily. "Now bring me a clean menu."

MAY 20

The maiden aunt was trying to promote good relations with her young nephew.

"I'll give you a quarter if you'll kiss me," she offered.

"A quarter?" he spurned. "Why, I get that for just taking a physic."

MAY 21

"Who wrote *Macbeth*?" asked the teacher of her class.

"Not me," snapped Sammy much to the class' amusement.

His joy, though, was short-lived when the teacher ordered him to bring his father to school.

Sammy's parent was up to the occasion.

"Listen," he told the teacher, "my boy, Sammy, is no

liar. He always tells the truth and if he says he didn't write *Macbeth* you can bet your bottom dollar he didn't do it."

That night the father proudly related the incident at home but Sammy's mother was not impressed.

"Dope!" she criticized her husband. "You should have told the teacher that maybe Sammy wrote it this time but from now on he'll be a good boy and never do it again."

MAY 22

"Who gave the bride away?" asked a latecomer to the wedding.

"Her little brother," was the reply. "Right in the middle of the ceremony he shouted, 'She finally landed him, didn't she, Ma.'"

MAY 23

When the tightwad heard that the doctor charged twenty dollars for the first visit and only ten dollars for everyone after that he stomped into the physician's office and bellowed, "Well, doctor, here I am again."

MAY 24

A customer in the restaurant asked a waitress if she served crabs.

"We serve anybody," she announced expansively.

MAY 25

"How much is this perfume?" a lady inquired of the department store clerk.

"Three hundred dollars an ounce," was the answer.

The customer was amazed.

"And just what do you call it?" she asked.

"'Perhaps,'" said the clerk.

That miffed the lady.

"For three hundred dollars an ounce," she snorted in return, "I don't want 'Perhaps', I want 'For Sure.'"

MAY 26

A well-known author took his friend to a comedy writer's convention as a guest. At lunch the first day the friend was surprised by some of the proceedings. Every so often someone would get up, mention a number and it would be greeted invariably with a big laugh.

"What gives?" he inquired of his host.

"Simple," said the author. "All jokes rely on a basic comedy situation that the professionals have numbered just to save time and energy. We all have the numbers memorized so that we always know what someone is talking about."

"Twenty-six," one of the writers announced at that moment and he was greeted with a loud guffaw.

"See what I mean?" the host remarked to his friend.

In a few minutes someone else arose and announced number fourteen but he was met with stony silence and that mystified the guest.

"What's happened now?" he asked. "How come that fellow didn't get any laughs?"

"Well," drawled the host, "some people just don't know how to tell a joke."

MAY 27

"Are you bothered by bad thoughts?" a psychiatrist asked his patient.

"Not at all," was the answer. "As a matter of fact I enjoy them. Immensely!"

MAY 28

"Who's Nora?" a wife asked her playboy husband one morning at breakfast.

"Some horse I bet on yesterday," he faked smoothly.

"That horse," slugged his missus, "is on the phone and wants to talk to you."

MAY 29

Said one mother kangaroo to another mother kangaroo, "I hate these rainy days when the children have to stay in and play."

MAY 30

"Your husband contends that being married to you makes him lead a dog's life," the judge told a woman in a divorce case.

"He's absolutely right, Your Honor," she agreed. "He comes into the house with muddy feet, takes the choice spot near the fireplace, waits to be fed, sleeps whenever he wants to, growls constantly, and always wants to be petted."

"Divorce granted," said the judge without further argument.

MAY 31

A well-known industrialist died after an extended Florida vacation that spanned an entire winter. The body was shipped back to his native Northern city for burial.

As his friends filed past for a last look in the funeral parlor one of them observed, "He sure looks wonderful, doesn't he."

Whereupon someone in the back snapped, "Why shouldn't he look good. He spent the whole winter in Florida, didn't he?"

LETTER OF THE MONTH

Land of Israel

Dear Miss History:

The Queen of Sheba is currently visiting me and I have become so impressed by her exquisite beauty that I simply must have her as my wife.

The trouble is, however, that I already have a thousand other wives and my ministers strongly advise me against acquiring still another one.

Please tell me what you think.

King Solomon

Your Majesty:

Listen to your ministers. You need another mother-in-law like a centipede needs another leg.

LIFE'S LITTLE PHILOSOPHIES

Nobody
   wears
      glasses
         on
            the
               back
                  of
                     their
                        heads
                           because
                         we
                           all
                             have
                         20/20
                           hindsight.

If
   some
      people
         weren't
            stupid
               how
                  would
                     we
                        know
                        who's
                           intelligent.

JUNE 1

A plastic surgeon did rather extensive work on a patient and when time came for a final check-up the doctor was disappointed with the results. Convinced that the truth was by far the best approach he told the patient's wife, "Frankly I don't like the way your husband looks."

"Neither do I," she cheerfully admitted, "but he's awfully good to the children."

JUNE 2

When a mother caught her little boy kissing the neighbor's small daughter she decided to put an immediate stop to it.

"You keep that up," she warned her son, "and you'll never get to Heaven."

"Heaven can wait," retorted the little boy. "This is Paradise."

JUNE 3

A hard fought ping pong contest had just been concluded when a newcomer appeared.

"Whose game?" he inquired.

"I am," replied a sweet young thing.

JUNE 4

A small town newspaper printed the following item. "Due to our shortage of paper a number of births will be postponed until next week."

JUNE 5

Years ago a bartender was very much annoyed with a moocher who came in every day exactly at noon and ate his fill of the free lunch without buying a single drink. Not only that but he compounded his dastardly trick by not even bothering to thank anyone for the privileges he enjoyed.

Soon the bartender, resenting the incident, plotted to get even with the moocher. He thought hard and long, explored every possible solution, asked advice in many quarters and finally came up with what he considered a good answer. He filled the free lunch counter with dog biscuits and awaited further developments with unquestioned glee.

The following day the moocher arrived on schedule and immediately began eating the biscuits with relish, wolfing down every last one and registering as much facial enjoyment as if he were partaking of a gourmet feast. The amazed bartender decided to wait another few days before drawing a conclusion but the same procedure took place again and again. Finally it became obvious that the moocher had won and the frustrated bartender conceded defeat and filled the lunch counter with the customary foods.

The next day when the moocher returned he took one look at the lunch counter and immediately roared, "Hey, bartender, where are those cookies?"

JUNE 6

"How would you like to die?" an eighty-five-year-old man was asked.

"Get shot by a jealous husband," was the immediate response.

JUNE 7

Mary, Mary, will you get up,
But Mary said, "I'm not able,"
Mary, Mary, you must get up,
We need the sheet for the table.

JUNE 8

A little girl was sobbing uncontrollably when a passing stranger, sorry for her, tried to comfort her.

"I wouldn't cry like that if I were you," he began.

"You cry your way," the child remarked, "and I'll cry mine."

JUNE 9

An employee had just been on a two week vacation and on the first day of his return he asked his boss for a couple of weeks off to get married. The employer denied the request and asked, "You just had two weeks off. Why didn't you get married then?"

"And spoil my vacation?" shouted the astonished employee.

JUNE 10

A customer in a restaurant ordered a gargantuan meal that was easily triple of what a normal person would eat and he consumed every morsel with relish.

His waitress watched him throughout the procedure and when he finished she observed admiringly, "You sure love food, don't you."

"It's not the food," he corrected, "it's just that I have a big yen for bicarbonate of soda."

JUNE 11

"My mother-in-law's been living with us for eight years and she's always causing trouble between me and my wife," a man complained to his friend.

"Get rid of her," advised the friend.

"Can't," was the frustrated reply. "It's her house."

JUNE 12

Three men were riding on a bus and as they neared the station the first man spoke up.

"Is—is—th—th—this P—P—Peoria?" he inquired of the second man.

The latter did not answer.

"I—I—s—s—say," repeated the first gent, "is th—th—th—this P—P—Peoria?"

The second man still kept quiet.

Unable to endure it any further the third man spoke up and said, "Yes, this is Peoria."

"Th—th—th—thank you, v—v—v—very much," said the first man as he got off.

After he was gone the third man spoke up again.

"Why didn't you answer him?" he inquired of the second gent.

"D—d—d—do you th—th—think I—I—w—w—want to g—g—g—get a p—p—punch in the n—n—n—nose?" was the reply.

JUNE 13

An actor willed that his body be cremated and that ten per cent of the ashes be thrown in his agent's face.

JUNE 14

This story has been making the rounds for decades. Two women met on the street.

"How's your daughter?" asked the first.

"Wonderful," said the second. "Couldn't be better. She made a marvelous marriage. She never gets out of bed before eleven o'clock, has breakfast served to her, plays cards all afternoon or visits with friends, eats dinner in the finest restaurants, sees nothing but the best shows, has a full-time maid and all the other help she needs."

"Isn't that lovely," remarked the first lady. "And your son?"

The pleasant expression on the second lady's face changed to one of severe disappointment.

"Terrible!" she moaned. "Just awful. He's saddled with a rotten wife. Never should have married her. She never gets up before eleven o'clock, insists on having breakfast served to her, wastes her time all afternoon playing cards or visiting with friends, has to eat dinner in nothing but the finest restaurants, must see all the best shows, has a full-time maid and all the other help she needs. My poor son!"

JUNE 15

A man complained to his doctor that he was losing his memory.

"I can't recall a thing," he recounted. "The minute I hear it I forget it. It doesn't make any difference what it is, either."

"How long has this been going on?" asked the physician.

"How long has what been going on?" asked the patient.

JUNE 16

The alcoholic gave his teetotaling wife a sip of his drink and she immediately reacted adversely. She gagged, she coughed and fought for her breath, and finally she managed to sputter, "How can you possibly drink such vile stuff?"

Assuming his most possible self-righteous stance he said, "See? And you always thought I was having such a good time."

JUNE 17

"If you were walking along the street," inquired a man of a very sedate lady, "and you saw a little worm would you pick it up?"

Practically abhorred, she snapped, "I should say not!"

"Honey," he chuckled, "you're no chicken."

JUNE 18

One very conceited actor carried on so at his wife's funeral that he convinced all those present he was totally heartbroken. At the conclusion of the services he was approached by many of the mourners who offered him their condolences.

"I know how badly you must feel all over this," one of them said to the thespian.

"Badly, nothing," he disagreed. "This is the best part I've had in years."

JUNE 19

He: Goodness, what a beautiful bracelet.
She: Goodness had nothing to do with it.

JUNE 20

The restaurant owner said to his head waiter, "Take care of things. I'm going out to eat."

JUNE 21

Walking into his favorite tavern with a new dog one evening a man announced to his friends that the animal was a rare specimen and that he was indeed fortunate to have just obtained him.

"What's so special about him?" he was asked.

Pulling himself up to his full height, with unquestionable pride, the man said, "This dog can talk. As a matter of fact he can talk as well as any human."

Total skepticism greeted him instantly and it was so overwhelming that he soon had to back up his contention with money and practically everyone in the tavern had bet him that the dog did not possess such unusual powers.

"This one time you are all wrong," the man told his

friends. "Too bad you're going to have to pay for the lesson."

Turning to his dog he commanded confidently, "Talk!"

There was utter silence!

"Talk!" the man repeated but still there was no response.

"Talk!" he shouted a third time but it was to no avail.

"Talk," he finally begged but the dog ignored him much to the amusement of everyone else in the tavern.

Exasperated the man realized he had lost and he paid off his debtors and left.

However, as he walked back to his apartment, sadder but possibly wiser, the dog broke the silence and said, "But after what happened tonight, think of the odds we can get tomorrow."

JUNE 22

An Englishman confided to his friend, "My wife threatens to leave me if I don't stop seeing other ladies."

"Too bad," consoled the chum.

"Yes," admitted the Englishman, "I'll certainly miss the old girl."

JUNE 23

"Call me a cab," a haughty matron ordered an innocent bystander as she emerged from her apartment building.

"Okay," complied the annoyed bystander, "you're a cab."

JUNE 24

Guilt-ridden over how badly he had been treating his wife of late the husband vowed to change his habits and make life more pleasant for her and prove how much he appreciated the wonderful wife and mother she was. Accordingly, he rushed home that evening earlier than usual laden with flowers, candy, and a bottle of champagne as proof of his altered intentions.

As he entered their home his wife took one look at him and was overcome. She was so overcome, as a matter of fact, that she burst into tears and began to sob hysterically.

"I broke my best dish today," she wailed, "the roof's leaking, the baby's running a fever, the car won't go and now, to top it all off, you come home drunk."

JUNE 25

Love is the tenth word in a telegram.

JUNE 26

"Your husband must have absolute rest and quiet," advised the doctor. "Here are some sleeping pills."

"How often should he take them?" asked the patient's wife.

"Oh, they're not for him," corrected the doctor. "They're for you."

JUNE 27

"That lady in the house next door is sure outspoken," a husband told his wife.

"By whom?" asked the missus icily.

JUNE 28

Walking into the lobby of a resort hotel where he and his family were vacationing a man was upset when he spied his daughter standing there with one of the guests who had his arm around her shoulder.

"You tell that young man to get his arm off you," he ordered sharply.

"Tell him yourself," the daughter replied just as sharply. "He's a perfect stranger to me."

JUNE 29

"Had to shoot my dog yesterday," an Englishman related.

"Was he mad?" asked the listener.

"He wasn't exactly pleased about it," was the candid reply.

JUNE 30

Two men had been doing business with each other for years and each had accepted the other's word as binding without resorting to any written contracts or other types of formal documents.

One day, however, upon closing a deal and presenting final payment, one of them demanded a written receipt. His friend was shocked.

"But we've been doing business for years," he pointed out, "and you've never doubted my word. Nor have we ever had any trouble. Why, after all this time do you suddenly want a receipt? Have I done something wrong? If there is, please tell me."

"No," said the other, "you've done nothing wrong. As a matter of fact everything is fine, same as always."

"Then why this sudden change?"

"Simply this," explained the first man. "You and I are getting along in years and life being as unpredictable as it is, one of us may pass on suddenly and eventually the other one will go too. When my time comes and I get to

Heaven I want to prove to Saint Peter that I led a decent life down here and that, among other things, I paid all my debts and don't owe anybody a cent. And when that time comes I don't want to have to run all over Hell looking for you just to get a receipt."

LETTER OF THE MONTH

New York City

Dear Miss History:

For many years I have heard a great deal of talk about the difference between the older generation and the people of today.

Frankly I prefer the oldsters. I still yearn for the so called good old days when the ladies fainted every time a gentleman kissed them. That, to me, was femininity personified, and it represented exactly the way a woman should respond.

Tell me, Miss History, just where are those girls of yesteryear.

Concerned

Dear Concerned:

And just where are the old fashioned men who made them faint.

LIFE'S LITTLE PHILOSOPHIES

If
  horses
    are
      dumb
        animals
          how
            come
              they
                never
              lose
                money
              at
                  the
                    track.

If
  you
    have
      a
        problem
        with
          your
            breath
            keep
          your
              mouth
              shut.

JULY 1

A group of mourners, having just laid to rest a close friend, were forced to walk back to town from the cemetery when their car broke down. One of them was ninety-five years old and progress for him was slow because of his infirmities.

Noticing the old man's dilemma a close friend whispered to him, "Not much point in your leaving here, is there."

JULY 2

Trying to impress a pretty elevator operator the young man started his conversation with, "I'll bet all these stops and starts make you tired."

"No," she yawned, "it's the jerks that really bother me."

JULY 3

Though they had been engaged over a year and were close to marriage the young couple had a stormy personality clash one day and broke up.

Shortly afterward they both accidentally attended the same party and their host, not aware of their prior relationship, introduced them to each other as if they were total strangers.

"I'm sorry," she faked icily, "but I didn't get the name."

"Nope, you sure didn't," conceded the former boy friend, "but nobody can say you didn't try."

JULY 4

The doctor presented his final bill to the executor of the estate of a patient who had recently passed on.

"Is it necessary to have this bill notarized?" he asked.

"No," replied the executor. "The fact that the patient died is proof enough that you attended him profession-ally."

JULY 5

The horse breeder crossed one of his animals with a giraffe as an interesting experiment. To his surprise he obtained an animal that was not too fast in a regular race but he proved to be terrific in a photo finish.

JULY 6

An opinion sampler conducted a survey that showed freight trains working at eighty per cent capacity while at the same time alcoholic consumption in humans had climbed to a new high of ninety-seven per cent.

"This proves," he concluded, "that people get loaded more often than freight cars."

JULY 7

A teacher penned the following note on the report card of one of her students.

"Elmer does well in his studies but he spends too much

time playing with the girls. I believe I have a plan that will cure him of this and would like your permission to try it."

The boy's mother signed the card and wrote back, "Permission granted and if the plan works be sure and let me know so's I can try it on his father."

JULY 8

The customer brought his automobile to the repair shop and insisted there was a defect in it. The mechanic carefully checked it over and found nothing wrong.

"As a matter of fact," he told the customer, "this car is in excellent shape."

Dissatisfied, the customer asked, "Then what's that knock I hear when I push it up to eighty?"

"That," was the quiet reply, "is probably the Good Lord warning you to slow down."

JULY 9

A bachelor, approaching middle-age, was courting a young lady and was successfully resisting every one of her attempts to get him to propose marriage. Finally, in desperation, she openly reminded him of his age and strongly advised him to marry before it was too late.

"Never," parried the bachelor self confidently, "I find that there's always enough fish left in the ocean."

"Maybe so," retorted the young lady, "but the bait gets stale after a while."

JULY 10

After treating the patient six months the psychiatrist advised him that he was finally cured of the delusion that he was Marc Antony.

"Wonderful," applauded the patient, "I just can't wait until I get home and tell Cleopatra."

JULY 11

During a discussion of Heaven and Hell a usually talkative individual maintained strict silence.

"How come?" he was asked.

"I've got friends in both places," he explained, "and I'm not about to offend anybody."

JULY 12

Eager to save money on a fight scene a Hollywood producer came up with a most unique gimmick.

"Jack," he told his star, "there's a couple across the street waiting for a bus. Go over and insult the woman. That will make her escort mad enough to punch you. Meanwhile we'll keep rolling the cameras and get a free fight scene out of it."

At first the star demurred but when he noted that his intended opponent was somewhat overweight and a little along in years he agreed.

Crossing the street he approached the couple in a rather casual manner and opened the conversation.

"Good day, sir," he began, "is that your wife?"

The husband nodded quietly.

"She is rather ugly, isn't she," continued the actor. "Doesn't have her makeup on right, her clothes show no taste, she looks awful."

With that the thespian braced himself for the first punch but instead there was a long silence as the husband looked at his wife with a very critical eye.

Finally he said to her, "See? That's exactly what I've been trying to tell you all these years."

JULY 13

The vacationer was anxious to go swimming but he knew nothing about the nearby waters. Having been warned about the possibility of undesirable animals he decided to check with a local bystander.

"The water sure looks good," he offered. "Any crocodiles in here?"

"No, sir," came the reassuring reply.

"Are you positive?" double checked the stranger.

"Absolutely," insisted the local. "They're afraid of the sharks."

JULY 14

When a top-notch gambler died all the members of his betting fraternity showed up for the funeral.

All went well until the minister in his final eulogy said, "This man isn't really dead. He's just asleep."

Whereupon a voice in the crowd, pointedly critical, shouted, "I've got ten big ones here that says he's dead."

JULY 15

A genealogist had done rather extensive research on the family tree of a wealthy client and had uncovered the embarrassing fact that one of the ancestors had been electrocuted for crimes against the state.

"I can't give a client any disturbing news like that," the genealogist confided to his partner. "He has a lot of influential friends and it could give us a black eye."

"Just tell him," advised the partner, "that the forbearer occupied the chair of applied electricity at a public institution."

JULY 16

An illiterate but beautiful young lady had a boy friend who wrote her voluminous letters whenever he was out of town. To solve her problem she had one of her neighbors read the letters to her.

"But," a friend pointed out to her, "that doesn't give you much privacy, does it."

"Sure it does," was the reply. "I make her stuff her ears with cotton so's she won't hear what she reads."

JULY 17

Joe had run up a bill for ninety-eight dollars at his favorite bar and was unable to pay it. Embarrassed, he stopped frequenting the place.

He was very popular, however, and many of the customers asked about him. Realizing it would be good publicity to have him back the bartender managed to contact Joe and invited him to return.

"As a matter of fact," he told him, "we'll just forget that ninety-eight dollar bill and start fresh."

Joe was pleased and agreed to return. On his first evening back the bartender took out Joe's tab and tore it up in front of the customer's eyes.

"That proves I'm sincere," he told Joe. "As far as I'm concerned the bill is paid in full."

Whereupon Joe pulled himself up to his full height, threw back his head authoritatively and inquired, "Isn't it customary for the house to set them up when a man pays his bill?"

JULY 18

A wife gave her husband a package.
"This is for your secretary," she directed.
"What is it?" asked the husband.

"Hair tonic."

"Hair tonic? But how do you know she needs it."

"Because I can see that her hair is coming out," said the missus, "all over your coat."

JULY 19

A man entered a police station and calmly laid down his gun on the sergeant's desk.

"I just shot my son-in-law," he announced evenly.

"Shot your own kin?" asked the surprised sergeant.

"Well," drawled the offender, "he wasn't my son-in-law when I shot him."

JULY 20

The tightwad gave his son a quarter to go to sleep, took it from him when the lad was in dreamland, and then spanked him the following morning for losing it.

JULY 21

"When people get married what do they say?" a little tyke asked his mother.

"They promise to love, honor, and cherish each other," was the reply.

"Then you and Daddy aren't always married, are you," was the sound observation from the youngster.

JULY 22

The doctor was surprised to find his patient drunk and in bed.

"If you had taken my advice," he admonished, "you wouldn't be in this predicament now."

"But I did take your advice," alibied the patient. "I

took whiskey and aspirin just like you prescribed."

Eyeing the patient critically the physician observed, "Looks to me like you got way ahead on the whiskey and way behind on the aspirin."

JULY 23

"Where I come from," said the dude from the East in an attempt to impress his Western saloon audience, "we call a spade a spade."

"Good idea," one of the cowboys complimented. "Last week one of the boys called a spade a club and we shot him."

JULY 24

During the days of the developing frontier justice was at times swift and final. One man, strongly suspected of theft, was sentenced to be hung.

His wife appealed to the judge.

"But you have no proof," she argued. "Do you mean you're going to hang my husband purely on circumstantial evidence?"

"Not at all," alibied the jurist. "We're just going to tie a rope around his neck and then shove him off the platform. From then on it'll all be up to him."

JULY 25

A bright young lady driving a new convertible suddenly turned a corner without any prior signal and smashed into another car.

When the victim extricated himself from the wreckage he managed to raise enough anger to demand of the lady, "Why didn't you signal you were going to turn?"

"Don't be silly," she replied. "I always turn here."

JULY 26

The artist was exhausted and his creative mind refused to function. Wearily he told his model to remain clothed.

"It's no use," he said. "This is just one of those days."

"I understand," she assured him. "Why don't you have a cup of coffee and try to relax. We can work again tomorrow."

"Good idea," he agreed. "How about joining me."

"Don't mind if I do."

The suggestion proved fruitful and they were both enjoying their respite when the artist happened to gaze out of his studio window and spied his wife coming up the walk.

"Quick!" he ordered the model. "Get undressed! It's my wife!"

JULY 27

A man stood before a grave muttering, "You shouldn't have died! You shouldn't have died!"

A passerby, deeply touched, asked, "Your wife?"

"No," was the answer. "Her first husband."

JULY 28

Little Charley had been a problem all day and his father was duly informed of it when he arrived home from the office that evening.

Calling his young son aside he asked him confidentially, "And just what would it take to make you a good boy?"

"One dollar," was the instant reply.

"One dollar?" echoed the astounded parent. "Why, when I was your age I was good for nothing."

JULY 29

"Seems to me Joe doesn't trust his wife anymore," one friend said to the other.

"How come?" was the natural query.

"Well," was the drawled reply, "last week after he left the house one morning he tiptoed around to the back, went into the kitchen, slipped up behind his wife and kissed her on the neck."

"And?"

"And without turning around she said, 'Okay, pal, just leave two scrubbing brushes and one clothes brush.'"

JULY 30

"I haven't worked a day in my life," the socialite bragged to the hard hat.

"You haven't missed a thing," was the rejoinder.

JULY 31

In an auto accident one of the victims was thrown so far away he was given a ticket for leaving the scene of the accident.

LETTER OF THE MONTH

St. Petersburg

Dear Miss History:

I know there are those who will disagree with me but on balance I have contributed a great deal to my country and to the royal family.

For example, I have effectively controlled the bleeding sickness of the Tsarevitch despite the objections of the medical profession. In another area I have provided peace and spiritual consolation for the Tsarina and, at times, even for the Tsar himself. I have also given my advice on political matters and they have been very astute if I must say so myself.

Despite that, my jealous enemies have accused me wrongfully of such misdemeanors as drunkenness, brawling and, especially, illicit love affairs. They are obviously trying to besmirch my reputation and belittle me in the eyes of those whose confidence I now enjoy.

I am afraid their lies may eventually harm me and it worries me constantly. What can I do?

Rasputin

Dear Lover Boy:

Forget the lies. Start worrying when they tell the truth about you.

LIFE'S LITTLE PHILOSOPHIES

While
  you're
    waiting
      for
        the
          right
           girl
            to
              come
               along
                have
                  fun
                    with
                      the
                        wrong
                          ones.

Fat
  people
    are
      good
        natured
          because
          they
            can't
              fight
              or
                run.

AUGUST 1

The motorist was caught speeding and when the police officer was writing out the ticket he protested vigorously.

"But I wasn't breaking the law," he insisted. "I know I wasn't. I kept a careful eye on the speedometer and it was exactly the same as the speed limit posted on the sign a mile back. I'm positive I wasn't breaking the law, officer."

The cop finally tired of the man's constant yakking and he snapped sarcastically, "Maybe you weren't breaking the speed limit but I'm going to reward you with a ticket for really trying."

AUGUST 2

The man seated at the bar was going through a number of odd gestures. Periodically he would laugh out loud. Occasionally he held up his hand in a halting motion. This went on for a while until the bartender became curious enough to find out what it was all about.

"Is anything wrong?" he asked the customer.

"Nothing at all," was the reply. "Frankly I'm enjoying myself."

"Then why all the motions?"

"It's this way," explained the customer. "I'm telling myself jokes. If they're good I laugh but if I've heard them before I hold up my hand to stop myself."

AUGUST 3

Little Jimmy's mother was unusually careful to keep her son clean. Daily she bathed, scrubbed, and groomed him almost to the point of pain. Jimmy's pain, that is.

Her efforts, however, did not go unnoticed and many a neighbor complimented her on her little son's appearance. This made her so proud that she became even more zealous in her work—much to Jimmy's chagrin.

One day a neighbor said to Jimmy, "My but you've grown a lot these last few months."

"Why shouldn't I," snapped the youngster, "from the way my mother's been watering me."

AUGUST 4

"This morning I saw a patient with a split personality," one psychiatrist related to another.

"How did you treat him?" asked the second physician.

"I told him to go chase himself," was the wisecracking reply.

AUGUST 5

The beautiful young lady was visiting the country for the first time and the farmer, attempting to be a genial host and to acquaint her with things rural, was taking her on a tour of his land.

As they walked through the pasture they came upon a cow who was rubbing noses with a bull. Aroused by the sight the farmer shyly hinted, "Sure wish I could do the same thing."

"Go ahead," encouraged the young lady. "It's your cow."

AUGUST 6

The young pianist had spent a number of years studying and finally came his big night when he made his debut at Carnegie Hall. Unfortunately the critics were not pleased with his efforts and they said so in their columns. Whereupon the pianist's manager offered the following alibi.

"My boy," he explained, "spent six years studying in Vienna, four years in Rome, and two in Paris. Actually, he spent so much time in those foreign countries he completely forgot how to read American music."

AUGUST 7

"How much do you charge for a haircut?" the tightwad inquired of the new barber.

"Four dollars," was the reply.

"And how much for a shave?"

"One and a half dollars."

"Then shave my head," ordered the thrifty one.

AUGUST 8

Two drunks at a dog show were admiring a rare species of dog whose face was completely covered with hair.

"Which end is which?" posed one of the inebriates.

"I don't know," said the other, "but I sure know how to find out."

"How?"

"Let's stick a pin in him and see which end barks," was the sagacious reply.

AUGUST 9

Said one kitten to another as they watched a tennis match one day, "My father's in that racket."

AUGUST 10

The ladies had just concluded a four hour meeting of their local bridge club. As a few of them were walking home they were discussing a new neighbor who had practically monopolized the meeting by spending almost the entire four hours talking about herself.

"Do you think everything she said was true?" asked one of the ladies.

"Impossible!" insisted her companion. "There just isn't that much truth in existence."

AUGUST 11

Three men were hailed before a cross-eyed judge.

"How old are you?" inquired the jurist of the first man.

"Twenty-three," responded the second.

"I wasn't talking to you," said the judge.

"I didn't say a word, Your Honor," insisted the third.

AUGUST 12

Moaning and groaning the patient limped into the doctor's office and begged for an immediate appointment.

"I'm terribly ill," he complained to the nurse. "My back hurts, my head aches, I have terrible pains in my chest, my stomach is upset and I have stabbing pains in my legs."

"Goodness," commented the nurse admiringly, "you must be awfully healthy to be able to stand all that pain."

AUGUST 13

Three storks were having a little confab during their local version of the coffee break.

"What do you do?" the first stork was asked.

"I take care of the ladies between thirty and forty years of age and believe me, it keeps me plenty busy," was the reply.

"How about you?" the second stork was asked.

"Oh, my job is to handle the ladies between twenty and thirty and the way things are these days I'm having all I can do just to keep up," the stork answered.

"And what is your assignment?" the third stork was asked.

"I scare the devil out of the high school kids," was the terse reply.

AUGUST 14

A husband and his not so clever wife were sitting in their living room watching television when the phone rang. The wife answered it.

She listened carefully for a few moments and then said, "It sure is."

With that she hung up and sat down.

"What was that all about?" asked her husband.

"The operator was on the line," the birdbrain explained. "She told me it's a long distance from New York and I agreed with her."

AUGUST 15

The police officer managed to stop a motorist who had been speeding at eighty miles an hour.

"What's the hurry?" the lawman needled. "You got an emergency or something?"

"Sure have," explained the excited motorist. "My brakes are bad and I've got to get home fast before I have an accident."

AUGUST 16

The troubled young man approached his minister.

"Is it right," he inquired, "for a man to profit by the mistakes of others?"

"Absolutely not," the minister assured him.

"Then," said the young man, "give me back the ten dollars I gave you two years ago for marrying me."

AUGUST 17

Then there was the traveling man who sent his wife a check for a hundred kisses on her birthday and she got one of the neighbors to cash it for her.

AUGUST 18

Creeping up behind a pretty girl a young man slipped his hands over her eyes and said, "If you can't tell me who it is in three guesses I'm going to kiss you."

"Okay," she giggled, "it's either George Washington, Patrick Henry, or Napoleon."

AUGUST 19

"I'm a self-made man," bragged a loud-mouthed nuisance.

"Obviously a case of labor shortage," noted a listener.

AUGUST 20

While waiting for a plane a man put a coin into a fortune telling machine merely for amusement. Out popped a card that read, "Your name is Bill Jones, you weigh one hundred and eighty pounds and you're waiting to catch the plane to Chicago."

He was stunned by such uncanny accuracy for the card was one hundred per cent correct. Puzzled as to how such an ingenious result was obtained he deposited a second coin to test the machine and find out if it was capable of repeating such an amazing performance. To his astonishment the second card was even more to the point and read, "Your name is Bill Jones, you weigh one hundred and eighty pounds and you are still waiting to catch the plane to Chicago."

This time he was unquestionably impressed but he was also intrigued. How could the machine be so faultlessly correct? The more he thought about it the more perplexed he became until he was finally lured into dropping a third coin to find out if the mysterious machine could make it three in a row.

Out came the card and this time it read, "That does it, stupid! Your plane to Chicago just took off."

AUGUST 21

"Doctor," a concerned woman complained, "my husband's mind has been wandering lately."

"Don't worry," the physician reassured her, "it can't get very far."

AUGUST 22

"They gave me a wonderful birthday party last night," one of the secretaries mentioned at the office the next day, "and they even had a big cake with twenty-one candles on it."

"Twenty one?" hissed a friend. "What did you do? Burn the candles at both ends?"

AUGUST 23

The old adage insists that necessity is the mother of invention. This was confirmed at church services one Sunday morning when the collection plate was passed around.

Attending the services was a well-known local skinflint and his two brothers. When the three gentlemen espied the approaching financial calamity they solved their problem when one of them fainted and the other two carried him out.

AUGUST 24

A laborer fell ten floors while working on a new building. After he landed a crowd gathered around him and one of the group was considerate enough to fetch him a glass of water.

That upset the victim even more than the accident.

"And how far does a man have to fall," he demanded, "before he rates a drink of whiskey?"

AUGUST 25

"Why can't you be as good as Doc Hunter's little boy?" a mother asked her six year old son.

"How can I," complained the little tyke. "Doc keeps the good ones for himself."

AUGUST 26

It was the young actor's first part in a show and he was new to the ways of show business. He only had a one line speech that consisted of, "Hark, I hear a cannon roaring."

During rehearsals no cannon was fired and the director supplied a sign for the young actor to indicate when it was time for him to deliver his little speech. The newcomer performed on cue and did well.

On opening night, however, the cannon was fired and the actor heard it done for the first time. Taken aback by the sudden noise he forgot himself completely and shouted, "What the hell was that."

AUGUST 27

"Does this train stop at Grand Central Station?" a passenger inquired of the conductor.

Convinced he was being ribbed, the official cracked, "If it doesn't there's sure going to be one terrific crash."

AUGUST 28

A young lady whizzed along the highway in an expensive new automobile and broke every traffic regulation imaginable. She exceeded the speed limit, crashed all the red lights, drove across double yellow lines, turned corners from the wrong lanes and completely disregarded all other traffic on the road.

A police officer finally brought her to a halt and demanded to see her license.

"License?" she stomped angrily. "How could I have a license when you people took it away from me last year."

AUGUST 29

A drunk was weaving his way out of a tavern when the president of the local temperance society saw him.

"I'm certainly sorry to find you coming out of a place like that," she admonished.

"What did you expect me to do?" the drunk quickly improvised. "Stay in there all night?"

AUGUST 30

"Tell me a story," a little girl begged of her mother one night.

"Wait till your father gets home," was the reply, "and he'll tell us both one."

AUGUST 31

An aggressive woman pushed her way to the head of the line at a butcher counter merely to ask for a pound of cat food.

Feigning courtesy she turned to the lady next to her and said, "I hope you don't mind my being waited on ahead of you."

"Not if you're that hungry," was the retort.

LETTER OF THE MONTH

Rome

Dear Miss History:

Years ago I pulled out a thorn from the paw of a suffering lion. The beast was grateful and has never forgotten me because of that.

To prove it I must relate to you that sometime later I was sentenced to be devoured by a hungry lion. When my time came it was that same lion that was released in the arena and sent to attack me. Luckily he recognized me and spared my life.

I was indeed fortunate. Since then the lion has attached himself to me and accompanies me wherever I go. He refuses to be parted from me but this, unfortunately, has become an embarrassment. People are afraid to come near me and it makes me very lonely.

What can I do?

Androcles

Dear Andy:

Change your brand of mouthwash.

LIFE'S LITTLE PHILOSOPHIES

A
chaperone
may
not
be
able
to
play
a
complete
game
anymore
but
she
still
knows
how
to
intercept
the
passes.

Love
  is
    like
      hash—
        you
          need
            confidence
           in
              it
                to
                  enjoy
                    it.

SEPTEMBER 1

After twenty years of seemingly wedded bliss a woman surprised the entire community by suing her husband for divorce.

"But I thought you were both so happy," the lawyer said when she approached him with the proposed action.

"That we were," she admitted.

"Then what happened so suddenly?" persisted the lawyer.

"Well," she explained, "every Saturday night for twenty years I washed that man's back."

"What's wrong with that?"

"Nothing," she replied, "except that last Saturday night when I went to wash his back it was already clean."

SEPTEMBER 2

Disgusted with the poor quality of his breakfast the customer complained to the waitress.

"These eggs are terrible," he began.

"Don't blame me," she objected. "I only set the table."

SEPTEMBER 3

"My wife has one of the worst memories in history," a man told his friend.

"Forgets everything?" asked the buddy.

"No," was the sad comment. "Remembers everything."

SEPTEMBER 4

A lady brought an old picture of her son to the photographers.

"I'd like to have it enlarged," she requested. "And could you please fix it so that he's not wearing that awful hat?"

"Of course," the photographer assured her. "But tell me, how does he part his hair? On the right or on the left?"

The woman searched her memory but couldn't recall.

"I'm not sure," she said, "but when you take off his hat you'll be able to see for yourself."

SEPTEMBER 5

"There's a fellow who's going places," a man pointed out as one of his neighbors passed by.

"Ambitious?" inquired his listener.

"No," was the reply. "His wife's out of town."

SEPTEMBER 6

The judge was tired of seeing the perennial alcoholic constantly appearing before him and he decided to make one more attempt to get to the source of the problem.

"Tell me," he encouraged, "just what is it that makes you drink so much?"

"Bad company," said the defendant glibly.

"Bad company?" questioned the judge.

"Yes, Your Honor," was the answer. "Every time I had a fifth the people with me were teetotalers."

SEPTEMBER 7

Two ladies met at a reunion. They had been rivals in the past and it was difficult for them to bury their differences.

"It's been almost ten years since we last met," remarked first lady. "I can see you've aged. I could hardly recognize you."

Not to be outdone the second lady immediately retorted, "I wouldn't have recognized you either except for your coat."

SEPTEMBER 8

Having just returned home from a date with her 85 year old boy friend a woman complained to her daughter that she had had to slap him three times during the course of the evening.

"Good Heavens," exclaimed the daughter. "Did he get fresh?"

"No," said the mother, "but each time I thought he was dead."

SEPTEMBER 9

Following an operation a patient came out of the anesthetic only to find the window blinds in his room still drawn.

"Raise them," he demanded.

"Sorry," the nurse declined, "it's against doctor's orders."

At the patient's insistence the physician was contacted and he explained, "Yes, I had those blinds kept down because there's a fire burning across the alley and I didn't want you waking up and thinking the surgery had been a failure."

SEPTEMBER 10

Once upon a time there was a father who despised actors and warned his daughter he would disown her if she ever married one. Of course the young lady soon fell in love with a thespian and pleaded her case passionately.

"Let me marry him," she begged her father.

"No," was the stern reply. "No actor will ever be part of my family and that's final."

"But, please," she persisted.

"No," he repeated. "Never."

"But you're making a hasty decision. You don't even know him."

"He's an actor and that's all I have to know."

"He's a wonderful man though. You ought to meet him. Once you get to know him I'm sure you'll change your mind."

"Not as long as he's an actor," insisted the parent.

The daughter, however, did not give up and she continued her pleas so ardently that her father finally consented to go to the theater and see the actor at work.

"He's not at all like what you think," she predicted.

Just to be scrupulously fair the parent sat through two performances. Then, convinced he had made the right decision he ran home and told his daughter, "You're absolutely right. He's not at all like what I thought. As a matter of fact you can marry the guy anytime. That ham's no actor and never will be."

SEPTEMBER 11

Two chorines were Christmas shopping.
"I wonder what I can get Gladys," mused the first.
"Why not get her a book," suggested the second.
"Naw," vetoed the first, "she's got a book."

SEPTEMBER 12

"Hear you buried your wife yesterday," a Yank remarked to an Englishman.
"Had to, old chap," replied the Briton. "She was dead, you know."

SEPTEMBER 13

A visitor appeared at a local jail and made a rare request.
"Show me the man who broke into my house last night," he said. "I want to find out how he did it without waking my wife."

SEPTEMBER 14

Proud of his appointment as the Queen's physician the professor announced it to his class by writing on the blackboard in large, bold letters the notice of his success. Under it in even larger and bolder letters was written, "God Save the Queen."

SEPTEMBER 15

After a wonderful two week vacation at a famous resort hotel with his wife the tightwad came to the cruellest of all blows—paying the bill. The itemized account that the desk clerk handed him was distressing.

"This is ridiculous," he exclaimed. "Look at all those charges. Especially this one! Two hundred dollars for meals. We never ate half of those meals."

"I'm sorry, sir," said the clerk, "but they were always available for you and we have to charge for them."

The thrifty one didn't like the explanation and he thought it over carefully. Finally an idea struck him.

"And how about the way you kept kissing my wife," he argued. "There ought to be a charge for that."

"But I did no such thing," the clerk shot back.

"But she was always available for you," countered the tightwad.

SEPTEMBER 16

"Bring me a steak," the customer ordered.

"Two dollar size or three dollar size?" inquired the waiter.

"What's the difference? Is one larger than the other?"

"No, sir," explained the waiter, "but with the three dollar one you get a sharper knife."

SEPTEMBER 17

Well aware of the difficulties the couple next door were having with their marriage a lady tactfully suggested to the wife that the best thing for her to do would be to seek a divorce.

"Divorce?" recoiled the wife. "I've been living with my husband for twenty years and now you want me to make him happy?"

SEPTEMBER 18

"Don't worry, doctor," the patient assured his psychiatrist. "I'll pay you the five hundred dollars I owe you or my name isn't Napoleon Bonaparte."

SEPTEMBER 19

Trying to find out if the young lady with whom he was dancing was seriously involved with anyone the gentleman asked, "Are you thinking of marrying anyone?"

"Yes," she instantly replied. "Anyone."

SEPTEMBER 20

"Do you have trouble catching colds?"
"Nope, they catch me."

SEPTEMBER 21

When her husband came home unusually glum one evening the wife asked, "What's the trouble, honey? Tough day at the office?"

"No," he said, "it's not that. It's the superintendent. He just bragged to me he's kissed every woman in this building except one."

"Yes," shot back the missus, "and I'll bet it's that snooty neighbor of ours next door."

SEPTEMBER 22

A prisoner recently admitted to the state penitentiary asked to see the warden at once.

"You better let me out of here right now," he warned the official, "because if you don't I'll corrupt everybody else that's in here. From what I've heard I'm the only one in the whole place that's guilty."

SEPTEMBER 23

The overzealous shoe clerk was anxious to make a sale.

"That's a lovely pair of shoes," he told the customer after he had helped her try them on.

"Yes," she admitted, "but they're much too tight."

"Everybody's wearing that kind this season," he pushed.

"Maybe so," she conceded, "but I'm wearing last season's feet."

SEPTEMBER 24

"What's a retainer?" a youngster asked his father.

"It's money you pay a lawyer before he does any work for you," explained the parent.

"Sort of like putting money into a gas meter before you get any gas, isn't it," concluded the youngster.

SEPTEMBER 25

"This is a most unusual piano," a woman bragged to her guests. "It can really tell time."

"Impossible," insisted one of her visitors and everyone else agreed with her.

"Skeptical, aren't you," countered the hostess. "Watch!"

Whereupon she started to play and before very long there was a loud banging on her wall and the voice of her neighbor was clearly heard to yell, "What's the matter with you? Don't you realize it's midnight?"

SEPTEMBER 26

On a tour of a mental hospital conducted by no less a person than the director several visitors came upon one of the patients who was jumping all over the lawn and cackling like a hen.

"Can't you possibly cure him?" one of the visitors asked most sympathetically.

"Certainly," the director insisted, "but we need the eggs."

SEPTEMBER 27

"My brother got a black eye just for kissing the bride," someone related.

"That's ridiculous," snorted a listener. "Kissing the bride is one of our oldest customs. Nobody hits you for that."

"Three years after the wedding?" asked the first man.

SEPTEMBER 28

A research investigator conducted a series of experiments in which he placed a cube of sugar at one end of the table and a fly at the other end. At a given signal he shouted, "Jump," and the fly immediately took off and landed on the sugar cube.

Next he introduced a variation in which he cut off the wings of the fly and when he yelled "Jump," there was no response from the fly. He repeated this procedure in fifty cases and in each one the response was the same. The fly did not move when he shouted.

Whereupon he wrote the following:

"In each case where the wings of the fly were removed the insect became stone deaf and did not respond to a shouted command."

SEPTEMBER 29

"Do you believe in the hereafter?" a foreman asked one of his employees.

"Sure do," was the positive reply.

"Then hereafter do what I tell you," said the foreman.

SEPTEMBER 30

The absent-minded professor put his wife outside and kissed the cat goodnight.

LETTER OF THE MONTH

High School

Dear Miss History:

Like many of my fellow students I am having a great deal of trouble with Latin. It's tough! We try hard but it's no use. We do well in the other subjects but when it comes to Latin we are licked.

What we want to know is how did the Romans ever master so difficult a language. What was the secret of their success? What did they do that we haven't done?

Please tell us. Maybe, if we know, we'll be able to do well in that subject too.

Average Student

Dear Average:

The Romans were born into it. If they had had to study Latin they would never have had time to conquer the world.

LIFE'S LITTLE PHILOSOPHIES

Man
  who
    proposes
      to
        a
          girl
            on
              the
                side
                of
              a
                  hill
                  is
                    not
                      on
                        the
                        level.

Success
  is
    relative.
    The
      more
        success,
          the
            more
              relatives.

OCTOBER 1

"My father was so smart," bragged one man, "that he knew the exact day he was going to die."

Unquestionably impressed, his friend asked, "How come?"

"The judge told him," was the answer.

OCTOBER 2

A patient was plagued by pain in one of his legs and he sought the advice of his physician.

"Why does it hurt so much, doctor?" he practically pleaded.

"It's your age," explained the doctor. "You're getting along in years and this is one of the things that happen with the passage of time."

The patient shook his head vigorously.

"Impossible!" he insisted. "My other leg is just as old and it doesn't hurt a bit."

OCTOBER 3

When a young man asked his former employers for a letter of reference he was supplied with the following.

"To whom it may concern: Mr. John Smith is leaving after having worked for us for three months. We are satisfied."

OCTOBER 4

"One of this chicken's legs is shorter than the other," a customer complained to the waiter.

To which the waiter responded, "You going to eat that chicken or dance with it?"

OCTOBER 5

"Who's being buried?" one man inquired of another while they were watching a funeral procession.

"Ben Green," was the solemn answer.

"Gosh," exclaimed the first, "is Ben dead?"

"Well," came the snappy comeback, "you don't think they're rehearsing with him, do you?"

OCTOBER 6

The perennial latecomer had been repeatedly reported to his supervisor. The latter, a firm believer in appealing to logical argument to make his point, called the offender into his office for a chat.

"Don't you realize you have to show a sense of responsibility if you want to advance?" he said to the latecomer. "You'll never get anywhere if you don't come to work early and the earlier the better."

The offender, however, was not impressed.

"You may be right," he granted, "but if you'll take a closer look you'll see that the guys who come to work early have to go to the guys who get here late to get paid."

OCTOBER 7

Severely injured in an automobile accident, the victim lay in the road writhing in pain as an excited crowd gathered. Someone, bursting with authority, pushed his way forward and took charge.

"Quick!" he ordered. "Somebody get some whiskey!"

It was the kind of a voice that produced rapid results and within moments the whiskey was produced. To everyone's amazement the authoritative one poured a big drink and gulped it down himself.

"That's better," he remarked with obvious relief. "I just can't stand seeing anyone suffer."

OCTOBER 8

Two people were trying to outdistance each other in spinning yarns about the coldest spot on earth.

"There's no place colder than Alaska," insisted the first.

"You ought to spend a winter in my home town in North Dakota," countered the second, "and you'll agree with me that it's the icebox of the universe."

Not to be outdone the first one said, "It gets so cold in Alaska that the instant you exhale your breath automatically freezes and your mouth is constantly covered with icicles."

"That's cold all right," admitted the second, "but in my home town we have a statue of George Washington in the public square and it has George with his hand on a little boy's head. Well, sir, it gets so cold there in the winter that George has to take his hand off the boy's head and put it in his pocket."

OCTOBER 9

The lady had been married four times and her husbands had included a millionaire, an actor, a minister and an undertaker.

Quipped an observer, "One for the money, two for the show. Three to make ready, and four to go."

OCTOBER 10

In applying for a job a girl inserted the following ad in the local newspaper.

"Would like employment as an elevator operator. Since I have no previous experience I would like to start in a low building."

OCTOBER 11

The newlyweds were having their first dinner at home. The young wife had spent the entire day in the kitchen carefully preparing each bite as if it were to be a gourmet feast. Every step was checked and rechecked before she was finally satisfied.

That night at the table she was too excited to eat and she sat on the edge of her chair closely watching her husband's reaction with every morsel he consumed.

Throughout the meal he said nothing and the wife's anxiety mounted. When he was finishing dessert she could stand the suspense no longer and she cautiously inquired, "If I keep cooking meals like this what will I get?"

"My insurance policy," he quietly responded.

OCTOBER 12

At the conclusion of the wedding ceremony the groom asked the minister to name his fee.

"Pay me what you think it's worth," the reverend said.

The new husband gave him a ten dollar bill.

The minister took another look at the bride and quickly gave the groom seven dollars change.

OCTOBER 13

"Sorry to hear your friendship with Jim ended when he ran off with your wife," a woman commented.

"That's not really broke us up," corrected the husband.

"No? What did?"

"He brought her back," was the answer.

OCTOBER 14

"I haven't seen you for three years," one man told another when they accidentally met on the street one day. "What have you been doing?"

"Three years," was the simple reply.

OCTOBER 15

When Al's fourth wife died his best friend, Charlie, called to offer his sympathy.

"I'm sorry about your loss," he told Al over the phone, "but, unfortunately, these things happen."

"I hope you won't take this amiss," Charlie went on, "but I won't be able to come to the funeral."

"Why not?"

Charlie, still married to his first wife replied, "Because I'm beginning to feel self-conscious since I won't be able to return the invitations."

OCTOBER 16

It wasn't the fall that hurt him. It was the stop on the cement that broke his neck.

OCTOBER 17

A big sale was advertised at a local store and a large crowd had collected even before the store was scheduled to open. As the minutes ticked away the line became longer and longer and the standees became increasingly impatient.

One small man, more impatient than the others, kept weaving in and out of the crowd until he had made his way to the head of the line when a husky, rough looking character grabbed him and shouted, "Back to the end of the line, Shorty, or I'll let you have it."

Completely cowed the small man returned to the rear but before long he was again inching forward until, once more, he came to the front spot. Once again, however, the rough guy spotted him and forced him to retreat.

Nevertheless the little fellow was determined. Disregarding the threats he repeated his performance although he did it cautiously. Unfortunately he wasn't cautious enough for his antagonist was too alert and caught him a third time.

"Listen, you little runt," the rough one bellowed, "I'm tired of your shenanigans and this time I'm really going to give it to you."

"You do," the little one warned, "and I won't even open the store."

OCTOBER 18

"Can you spare a quarter for a cup of coffee?" a hobo asked of a passing lady.

"Certainly not," demurred the lady. "Besides, what's a big strong man like you doing panhandling? Why don't you get a job?"

The hobo was horrified.

"And pay taxes to support a bum like me?" he recoiled. "No, thanks!"

OCTOBER 19

"That new doctor down the street is so considerate," a lady told her neighbor, "that if you can't afford an operation he touches up the X-rays for you."

OCTOBER 20

A rather quiet and unassertive man was driving along the highway while both his wife and his mother-in-law sat in the rear seats and shouted conflicting instructions to him. Accustomed to silent suffering he endured his ordeal for a long time without any retaliation.

Finally, however, he actually reached the limit of his patience and his meek soul rebelled. Turning around he faced his two tormentors, vigorously poked a finger at his wife and demanded, "Now let's get this settled once and for all. Who's driving this car? You or your mother?"

OCTOBER 21

A tightwad invited another tightwad to breakfast one morning and asked him how he would like his eggs.

"With ham," was the instant reply.

OCTOBER 22

When her five year old son came home with his father that afternoon the mother asked the little fellow, "And did Daddy take you to the zoo just like he promised?"

"He sure did," the boy confirmed happily, "and one of the animals came in first and paid four to one."

OCTOBER 23

The manager of a famous nightclub relied exclusively on the reactions of a pet parrot to reach his decision about the various entertainers that played his club. Perched on a railing that was specially constructed for him near the stage the bird would flap his wings enthusiastically if he liked the act. If he didn't he maintained a strict silence.

One night two actors were knocking themselves out trying to turn in a top-notch performance while their wives watched them from a front table. Suddenly one of the actors nudged his partner and whispered, "Hey, some drunk at the next table is kissing your wife."

"The devil with that," snapped the irate partner. "Just keep your eyes on that darn parrot."

OCTOBER 24

A man had just fallen off the bus.
"Have an accident?" a passing lady asked.
"No, thanks," he needled back, "I just had one."

OCTOBER 25

A young man asked his girl friend's father for her hand in marriage.

"Can you support a family?" inquired the parent.

"Certainly," the young man assured him. "I have an excellent job and my chances for further advancement are the best."

"Wonderful!" beamed the father. "Because there are five more of us besides my daughter."

OCTOBER 26

Convinced of his worldly sophistication the dapper Beau Brummel was squiring a lady home on what was their first date. In an obvious attempt to impress her he said, "I never bother with a girl unless she's had some experiences."

Awed by his overbearing presence the scared little girl said, "But I haven't had any experiences yet."

To which the mighty one quipped, "You're not home yet, either!"

OCTOBER 27

A potential customer entered a clothing store and inquired about the price of a new suit.

"Two hundred dollars," he was told.

"But," he protested, "that clothing store just across the way wants only one hundred dollars for the very same suit."

"Then why didn't you buy it?"

"He didn't have my size."

"In that case," observed the proprietor, "if you'll return when I don't have your size either I'll let you have that suit for fifty dollars."

OCTOBER 28

And then there were the sardines who objected to being packed in like commuters.

OCTOBER 29

Plagued with a toothache a member of a youth gang sought dental aid.

"Which tooth is bothering you?" the dentist asked.

"Find out for yourself," was the comeback. "I'm no stool pigeon."

OCTOBER 30

"You ought to pull down your shades," a man advised his friend. "Last night I saw you kissing your wife."

"This time you're wrong," said the friend. "I wasn't even home last night."

OCTOBER 31

A horse walked into a tavern and ordered a martini with a cherry in it. Downing it in one gulp he paid his bill and left.

"That's odd, isn't it," observed a barfly.

"Naw," corrected the bartender, "he always takes a cherry with his martini."

LETTER OF THE MONTH

Paris, France

Dear Miss History:

I have finally uncovered a wonderful formula for curing the sick especially the ones with functional problems. It is simple but effective and I am writing you in the hope that you will give my work the widest possible circulation.

The entire procedure consists of repeating a few chosen words over and over and those words are, "Day by day, in every way, I'm getting better and better."

As you can see there is no special preparation required nor is it necessary to interfere with one's daily routine to take advantage of this remarkable power of suggestion. The words can be repeated any number of times and at any time of day. Easy, isn't it.

Emil Coue

Dear Doc:

That's fine for the days but how about the nights.

LIFE'S LITTLE PHILOSOPHIES

Money
    isn't
        everything.
            You
                can't
                    buy
                        poverty
                            with
                                it.

Puppy
    love
        is
            the
                beginning
                    of
                        a
                            dog's
                                life.

Married
    men
        have
            better
                halves.
                    Bachelors
                        have
                            better
                                quarters.

NOVEMBER 1

Eager to gain quick rapport with a group of friends that he was addressing at a meeting, a business executive began his speech with this startling sentence:

"My dear friends. I won't call you ladies and gentlemen as I know you too well for that."

NOVEMBER 2

A poster along the highway read, "Are you prepared to meet your Maker?"

Right next to it was another large poster that announced, "Use Z-24. It's the best ointment for burns."

NOVEMBER 3

Three oldsters were fantasizing about their future.

"When I die," said the first, "I want to meet George Washington. There's a real hero. Father of our country, soldier, President—he's the best we've ever had."

"Washington was great all right," agreed the second, "but I want to meet Abe Lincoln. What he went through to keep our country together makes him one of the top men of all time."

Both men then turned to the third oldster and asked,

"How about you. Who would you like to meet in the Hereafter?"

"That cute blonde trick that works behind the candy counter at the department store," he said.

"But she's not dead," one of the others pointed out.

"Neither am I," he pointedly reminded them.

NOVEMBER 4

When Walt expired many of his drinking buddies showed up for the funeral services to pay their final respects to a man with whom they had imbibed over many a happy hour. During the past years he had been a most steady customer at the local beer parlors and made numerous acquaintances with his free spending ways.

The minister was moved by the large turnout and it stimulated him into embellishing his speech and talking of the departed man as a wonderful father, a most attentive husband, a model of charity, and a pillar of strength to the community in general. It was indeed a different picture of Walt from what he had actually been.

Puzzled by this sudden mention of virtue and dedication in a man who had been self-indulgent and largely irresponsible, the long suffering widow nudged her ten year old son and whispered to him, "Go up there and look into the casket again. I want to be doubly sure it's your father that's lying there."

NOVEMBER 5

Out of five thousand votes cast for sheriff one of the candidates received only fifty votes. He was not only the victim of a landslide, he was virtually annihilated. No other candidate in the entire history of the county had ever been so completely defeated.

The day after the election the unfortunate loser walked

down Main Street with two guns strapped to his belt, obviously ready for any eventuality. A fellow townsman stopped him.

"It's against the law to tote guns," the loser was told.

"I know," the defeated candidate admitted, "but when a man has as few friends as I have it's downright suicide to walk around unarmed."

NOVEMBER 6

When a researcher received a brochure from a hotel saying that the building contained a hundred guest rooms and eighty five baths he immediately concluded that fifteen of the guests are always dirty.

NOVEMBER 7

The very latest in refinement was achieved when St. Bernard dogs began travelling in pairs with one carrying the whiskey and the other the soda.

NOVEMBER 8

The ultimate modern agony occurred when a man rushed into an automobile agency and shouted, "Quick! Sell me a car! I just found a parking space."

NOVEMBER 9

The professor had talked extensively on kindness and he felt he had really extended himself to impress his class with the importance of such an outstanding virtue in our everyday lives. Anxious to find out if his students had absorbed much of the material he asked one of the pupils, "If I saw a man beating his donkey and I made him stop

132

what virtue would I be demonstrating?"

"Brotherly love," was the snappy reply.

NOVEMBER 10

The lady was celebrating her birthday and she had invited a number of close friends to help her celebrate the happy event.

"Wonderful party," complimented a close friend. "All birthdays should be like this."

"Yes," agreed the hostess, "but I hate to think of being thirty years old."

"Why," heckled the supposed pal. "What happened on that day?"

NOVEMBER 11

A wife sued her husband for divorce and when the case came to court the judge asked the little lady, "Why do you want to dissolve the marriage?"

The wife immediately poured out her resentment in a steady stream as if she had been waiting for just such a moment.

"That man is no good," she insisted. "Absolutely unreliable. All he ever thinks about is horses. Every chance he got he ran off to the races. At home all he ever read was the racing form. He'd never talk. We never went anywhere. We had no social life. As a matter of fact we had no life of any kind because it was nothing but horses, horses, horses. I'll bet you, Your Honor, that that man can't even tell you the day we were married."

That upset the defendant so much that he immediately blurted out, "I can too, Your Honor. We were married on the day Carry Back won the Kentucky Derby."

NOVEMBER 12

The patient was determined to learn the true extent of his condition.

On his next visit to the physician he demanded firmly, "Doctor, just what exactly is wrong with me and please don't use any of that fancy professional talk. I want straight facts."

The doctor believed him and replied, "You're just plain lazy."

Taken aback by such open frankness the patient retracted his courage and said, "Perhaps you'd better give me the scientific name for that condition, something I can use on my friends."

NOVEMBER 13

The little fellow was reciting his prayers very dutifully before going to bed.

"Dear Lord," he said, "please take care of Daddy and Mommy and Brother Will and Sister Jennie and Cousins Alfred and Benjamin and please Lord, please take extra good care of yourself because if anything happens to you we're all sunk."

NOVEMBER 14

The husband's final days had been pathetically painful and when death came it was considered by many to be a merciful release.

In choosing a headstone the widow was convinced that, under the circumstances, she was providing the proper touch with an inscription that read, "At Peace. Until we meet again."

NOVEMBER 15

"Daddy,"a bright little girl related to her father, "a baby was fed elephant's milk and gained ten pounds in one week."

Amazed, the parent inquired, "Whose baby is it?"

"The elephant's," was the innocent reply.

NOVEMBER 16

A visiting Texan was taken to a spot in the Swiss mountains where his local host tried to impress him by emitting a loud cry that returned as an echo a full fifteen minutes later.

"Isn't that terrific?" bragged the native.

The Texan was unaffected.

"Shucks," he downplayed, "that ain't nothing. Where I come from I lean out of my window just before I go to sleep and I yell, 'Time to get up.' Eight hours later the echo comes back and wakes me. That, sir, is what I call an echo."

NOVEMBER 17

"This is an unusual parrot," the pet shop owner told a prospective customer. "Raise its right leg and it sings, *Annie Laurie*. Raise its left leg and it warbles, *Sweet Adeline*. How's that for a rare bird?"

The customer was duly impressed but he wanted to explore all other possibilities.

"And what happens," he inquired, "if I pull up both legs at the same time?"

To which the parrot cracked, "I fall on my tail, stupid!"

NOVEMBER 18

Little Jimmy was very critical of his mother.

"I don't think she knows very much about children," he remarked. "She makes me go to bed when I'm wide awake and then when I'm fast asleep the next morning she wakes me up."

NOVEMBER 19

The mother of the dead man looked accusingly at her daughter-in-law as the cortege was wending its way to the cemetery.

"You drove my son to his grave!" she cried.

"Did you expect him to walk?" challenged the annoyed widow.

NOVEMBER 20

After Len had made a fortune and purchased a luxurious home he invited his old friend Ed for a visit. He took Ed on a tour of the entire place, went from room to room and carefully extolled all the expensive additions. Ed was flabbergasted by the lavishness of it all particularly when his old friend revealed not one but three swimming pools.

"But why three?" asked the astonished buddy.

"It's the only way I can take care of all my friends," Len carefully explained, "and still not offend anyone."

"I don't get it," said Ed.

"It's like this. Pool number one has only hot water in it for those who like to swim in higher temperatures. Pool number two has only cold water for those who prefer it that way."

"But," observed Ed, "pool number three doesn't have any water in it at all."

"That," said Len, "is for those who hate the water."

NOVEMBER 21

"Your big trouble is that you don't assert yourself," the psychiatrist told the henpecked husband. "You have to impress people with your importance. Especially at home. Tonight when you go home, bang your fist on the table, speak up firmly and loudly and tell your wife who's boss."

"Don't have to," said the meek hubby. "She already knows."

NOVEMBER 22

"Your boy is awfully forgetful," the teacher reported to the student's mother.

"Yes, he is," agreed the parent. "That's because when he was a child he had water on the brain. Now, every winter, it freezes and everything slips his mind."

NOVEMBER 23

A stranger rushed into a tavern and shouted excitedly to the bartender, "Quick, give me a drink before the trouble starts."

The bartender, always willing to help, hurriedly obliged

Swallowing it in one gulp the stranger said, "Better make it another one before the trouble starts."

Again the bartender poured a drink and again the stranger downed it instantly.

When he urged the bartender to pour a third drink, however, an element of curiosity was aroused and the bartender asked, "Just when is this trouble going to start?"

"Right now," admitted the stranger. "I can't pay for these drinks."

NOVEMBER 24

A young man who had made a habit of attending wakes and posing as a close friend of the departed gave such a convincing performance on one occasion that he was complimented by the dead man's wife.

"You must have been a wonderful friend to my husband, rest his soul," observed the widow.

"That I was," lied the imposter. "That I was."

"We simply can't decide whether to bury him or cremate him," she revealed. "I thought that since you were so close to him you might have an idea on the subject."

"Stuff him," the young man advised as he reached for another plate of food, "and let's keep the party going."

NOVEMBER 25

When informed by her clergyman that man was consigned to work out his salvation by the sweat of his brow the haughty dowager shot back, "Sweating is plebian. My family perspires."

NOVEMBER 26

Told that he was suffering from a very serious illness the patient tremulously asked his physician, "Do I have any chance of making it, doctor? Any chance at all?"

"Absolutely," the doctor quickly assured him. "Statistics show that nine out of every ten patients succumb to this particular malady but since you are the tenth I've seen this year with this disease and since the other nine have already passed on I'm sure you'll be all right. Guaranteed."

NOVEMBER 27

"Ever seen a lie detector?" one man asked another.
"Seen one?" exclaimed the second. "I married one."

NOVEMBER 28

"Give till it hurts," encouraged a young lady who was taking up a collection for a worthy cause.
"Madam," the tightwad replied, "the very idea hurts."

NOVEMBER 29

A man with a large family was walking down the street when a police officer stopped him and placed him under arrest.

"But why?" demanded the perturbed citizen. "I didn't do anything."

"You must have," insisted the cop, "otherwise that large crowd wouldn't be following you."

Which no doubt falls into the category of circumstantial evidence.

NOVEMBER 30

A successful executive was imparting the secrets of his prosperity to his employees.

"Determination is the real key to success," he told them. "It's that old never say die spirit that really pays off. Years ago I had a lot of bad luck and lost every nickel I had. Yes, I did. But did I give up? Did I surrender just because of a bad break?

"Not on your life! No, sir! I made up my mind that I would never let circumstances defeat me. I rolled up my sleeves, dug in my heels, gritted my teeth, put my shoulders to the wheel and borrowed another ten thousand dollars from my father-in-law."

LETTER OF THE MONTH

Vienna, Austria

Dear Miss History:

For many years I worked hard to develop the concept of the unconscious in Psychiatry.

Because I interviewed my patients while they reclined on couches in order to have them more relaxed and able to reveal themselves I became derisively known as a mind reader and my work was wrongly advertised as if it were a sideshow attraction at a carnival.

I frankly resent such an irresponsible distortion of the truth. It is, at best, a crude misrepresentation that should be stamped out and those who are guilty should be brought to strict account. Such misdeeds should not go unpunished and nobody, but nobody, should be permitted to malign innocent people so promiscuously. Don't you agree?

Dr. Sigmund Freud

Dear Dr. Freud:

Don't look now but your hostility is showing.

LIFE'S LITTLE PHILOSOPHIES

Marriage
is
like
a
prizefight.
The
preliminaries
are
better
than
the
main
event.

The
biggest
worry
in
this
world
is
not
money
but
the
lack
of
it.

DECEMBER 1

It was a Sunday afternoon and a young man decided to take his new girl friend into the country for a ride in an old-fashioned horse and buggy. When they were about five miles outside the city limits on a lonely road the horse suddenly dropped dead.

The young man was alert enough to recognize opportunity when it was so unexpectedly tossed to him and he immediately made ardent advances to his companion but she fought him off.

"You don't know what you're missing," he urged. "One of my kisses will put new life into you."

"Then kiss the horse," she snapped, "and let's get out of here."

DECEMBER 2

The young lady had been properly disciplined by her parents for coming in late. Wondering who had informed them of the time she came home she challenged the housekeeper who had actually seen her arrive.

The housekeeper, though, denied any responsibility.

"No, ma'am," she insisted, "I never did tell your parents when you got home. As a matter of fact I told them I was too busy cooking breakfast to notice the clock."

DECEMBER 3

He was so unreliable that if he lived in a harem he'd still play around with a girl on the outside.

DECEMBER 4

"What did you give your dog when he had distemper?" one farmer asked another.

"Turpentine," was the reply.

A week later when both men met again the first rustic said, "I took your advice but my dog died."

"So did mine," the second farmer sadly admitted.

DECEMBER 5

"Congratulations, Tommy," a neighbor said to a small boy. "I hear you've got a new baby brother."

"He's not so new," complained Tommy. "From the way he cries he must have had lots of experience."

DECEMBER 6

"Son," demanded an irate father, "just how did those long blonde hairs get on the back seat of my car?"

"I can give you an explanation," stuttered the embarrassed youth.

"Explanation, nothing," snapped the parent. "I want an introduction."

DECEMBER 7

"You'll never convince me there's a Hell," an atheist insisted to his girl friend.

"Just marry me," she challenged.

DECEMBER 8

"Last night I dreamed I was walking down the avenue with nothing on except my hat and was I embarrassed," a woman related to her psychiatrist.

"Embarrassed?" repeated the doctor.

"Absolutely. It was last year's hat."

DECEMBER 9

Three inmates of the state penitentiary were sentenced to be executed late in November. On the appointed day the warden visited each prisoner and solicitously inquired what they wanted for their last meal on earth.

"A thick, juicy steak with fried potatoes, string beans, apple pie, and a big dish of ice cream," requested the first prisoner.

"Half a fried chicken with mashed potatoes, gravy, hot biscuits, a big cut of cheese cake, and plenty of hot coffee," said the second.

The third inmate's order was very simple.

"Just a small dish of fresh strawberries," he asked.

"But fresh strawberries aren't in season right now," the warden pointed out.

"That's all right," was the quiet remark. "I don't mind waiting."

DECEMBER 10

"This hurts me as much as it hurts you," the father informed his young son as he spanked him.

"Maybe so," conceded the little tyke, "but not in the same place."

DECEMBER 11

"You know," a young man related to his girl friend, "two angels were talking about a recent survey where the results showed that ninety-five per cent of women on earth had poor morals."

"I don't doubt it," said the girl friend, "the way everybody is carrying on these days."

"One of the angels," continued the young man, "then suggested that they contact those ninety-five per cent and try to influence them to mend their ways."

"Good idea," said the girl friend.

"The other angel didn't think so," reported the young man, "because she felt it would be too tedious a job and instead she recommended they send a letter to the remaining five per cent. After some discussion it was agreed and do you know what they said in that letter?"

"No," said the girl friend. "What?"

"Oh," commented the young man innocently, "you didn't get a letter, did you?"

DECEMBER 12

When one of his better employees came in downcast one morning the boss asked him what was wrong.

"It's my wife," the employee sadly reported. "Last night when I went home and opened the door I found her and my best friend making love on the sofa."

"That is serious," conceded the boss and he spent quite a bit of time trying to console the employee.

The following morning, however, the same employee came to work with a big grin on his face.

"I solved my problem," he announced happily. "I sold the sofa."

DECEMBER 13

"I wouldn't vote for you if you were St. Peter himself," the disgusted voter told the politician.

"If I were St. Peter," countered the politico, "you couldn't possibly vote for me. You wouldn't be in my district."

DECEMBER 14

Two women were seated on a crowded bus.

"When we come to our stop," one said to the other, "we'll have to get off backwards."

"Backwards?" repeated her amazed companion. "Why?"

"See those two men standing in front of us?" whispered the first woman.

"Yes."

"I heard one of those men tell his friend that the moment we got up they would pinch our seats."

DECEMBER 15

Four salesmen were seated in the outer reception room of a company that was well-known for its prejudices.

Introducing himself to the others the first man announced, "My name is Gilson."

"Mine's Gatson," said the second.

"Glover," added the third.

"Also Ginsburg," summarized the fourth.

DECEMBER 16

"I expect to be married by the time I'm thirty," said one lady.

Quipped her friend, "I don't expect to be thirty until I'm married."

DECEMBER 17

"Cut down on your food and smoke one cigar a day," a doctor advised his patient.

"But—," the patient started to say.

"I mean it," interrupted the doctor. "Your health is the most important thing you have and if you don't follow my advice to the letter you'll be in for serious trouble and it will be your own fault."

Squelched, the patient went home and did exactly as he had been told. After all, he decided, the doctor knows best.

When he returned for a checkup a month later the doctor asked him for a full report.

"I'm doing okay on the food," he announced, "but that one cigar a day is killing me. I never smoked in my life."

DECEMBER 18

"You say your husband died of a broken heart?" a lawyer inquired of a bereaved widow who wanted to become his client.

"That's right," she confirmed. "If he hadn't broken my heart I wouldn't have shot him."

DECEMBER 19

Jim came home one pay day drunk and broke.

"I bought something for the house," he quickly alibied.

"What?" demanded his wife.

"A round of drinks," he replied.

DECEMBER 20

Will was a man of habit. Every Thursday was his night out and it never varied.

One Thursday, however, he left the house and failed to return. For three long years nobody heard from him despite numerous inquiries.

One afternoon, without any previous announcement, Will walked into the house. His wife was so elated by his return that she hurriedly called all their friends and invited them to a party that night.

"But why?" demanded the husband. "Why a party?"

"Because I'm so happy you're back home that I want all my friends to share my good fortune with me," his wife explained.

"But tonight's Thursday," Will objected, "and it's my night out."

DECEMBER 21

"How come you're still on crutches three months after your accident?" a man was asked. "Any complications?"

"Yes and no," was the honest reply. "I don't think I need them anymore but my lawyer says that since it was a city bus that hit me I better use them a while longer."

DECEMBER 22

"I whistle at every woman regardless of her age," one Lothario once explained. "If they're young they expect it and if they're old they appreciate it."

DECEMBER 23

The teenager was wearing a very abbreviated bathing suit and a police officer stopped her. Eager to impress on her young mind that she was in the wrong the officer said,

"I'm sure your mother would have plenty to say if she saw you in that suit."

"She sure would," confirmed the teenager. "It's her suit."

DECEMBER 24

It was Christmas eve and the thought of buying presents for his entire family made the skinflint miserable. He brooded hard and long and finally he stumbled on a solution.

He went out into his back yard and fired his gun. Then he reentered the house and announced to his family that Santa Claus had just committed suicide.

DECEMBER 25

Paris, France

Dear Miss History:

Jeanne du Barry is an exotically beautiful lady who has intrigued me very much. I have given her an honored place at my court and I find our relationship most enjoyable.

My friends, however, have criticized me. They point out that I am much older than Jeanne and that she and I represent the unrewarding combination of May and December. Specifically they have challenged me to explain what the freshness of her May can find in the wintry chill of my December. What can I tell them?

Louis XV, King of France

Your Majesty:

What can May find in December? Christmas, pal, Christmas.

DECEMBER 26

An eighty-five year old man was asked how he would like to die if he had the choice.

"Get shot by a jealous husband," he instantly replied.

DECEMBER 27

A motorist had just been unusually careless in his driving and had unfortunately caused an accident. What was more unfortunate was that he had struck a police cruiser and the officer involved had difficulty maintaining his temper.

"Okay," he snapped at the motorist, "just why did you make such a dumb mistake?"

Pointing to his wife who was in the rear seat the motorist shakily stammered, "She fell asleep."

DECEMBER 28

The confirmed alcoholic had been dating a young lady for over ten years and still there was no indication of any forthcoming wedding. The lady's father finally decided to bring matters to a head. Confronting the alcoholic one night he inquired directly, "Why haven't you and my daughter married yet?"

Replied the inebriate, "Every time I get drunk she refuses to marry me and then when I sober up I don't want to marry her."

DECEMBER 29

The patient had been very ill and almost every one had despaired of his life. He had actually lapsed into a coma and had remained in that condition for several days.

One morning he finally came out of it, opened his eyes,

looked around his hospital room and was still so disoriented that he asked weakly, "Where am I? In Heaven?"

His wife who had remained faithfully by his bedside throughout the entire ordeal replied, "No, dear. I'm still with you."

DECEMBER 30

"You ask me if this hair tonic is good?" the salesman said to the prospective customer. "Well, sir, let me tell you just how good this hair growing medicine really is. It's the best ever. It's accomplished miracles the likes of which you have never heard. It's absolutely terrific! As a matter of fact it's so terrific—let me just tell you what this tonic has accomplished. Back home we had a cat that had a rare kind of disease. It had lost every single hair on its body and was as bald as the proverbial billiard ball.

"That very same cat was sitting on the kitchen table one day doing nothing but licking its paws. I took one look at that unfortunate little animal and decided to do her the biggest favor of her feline life. I took the contents of this very bottle of the hair tonic and just poured them right on that wonderful cat.

"Well, sir, my sudden action caught that fine little animal by such surprise that she jumped right off the table. And do you know something? This terrific medicine worked so fast that before that cat got to the floor every single hair on its body had already grown back."

DECEMBER 31

HAPPY NEW YEAR.

LETTER OF THE MONTH

Troy

Dear Miss History:

I am the most beautiful woman in the world. Not only have individual men fought over me but at present there is a war in progress between the Trojans and the Greeks because a Trojan prince stole me away from my Greek husband.

I am flattered, of course, but I am also worried. Though I am the envy of the entire world I know that time will eventually take its toll and the future will bring many disappointments. My beauty will fade and men will no longer seek me. In ten more years life will have passed me by. What do I do then?

Helen of Troy

Dear Sex Appeal:

Skip the worries. You've got it made because in ten years you will look just as beautiful as you do today but it will take you longer.

LIFE'S LITTLE PHILOSOPHIES

If
  it
    weren't
      for
        marriage
          husbands
            and
              wives
                would
                  be
                    fighting
                      with
                        strangers.

He
  who
    laughs
      last
        didn't
          see
            the
              joke
                in
                  the
                    first
                      place.

LAUGH!
The
life
you
enjoy
may
be
your
own.

CABBY
By Leonard Jordan

PRICE: $1.95   BT51466
CATEGORY: Novel (Original)

Here are the compelling, hilarious revelations of a
New York City taxi driver. Arnold Shumsky knows
the city like the palm of his hand. He sees life
through the windshield of his cab from the dusk-to-
dawn hours when he plies his trade. He's a free-
lance knight errant on a Checker charger, looking
for dragons to slay and maidens to ravish.

ASTROLOGY
FOR THE WORKING GIRL
By Paige McKenzie

PRICE: $1.95 BT51467
CATEGORY: Non-fiction

In this practical guide, Paige McKenzie combines her extensive business experience, her knowledge of astrology and her good humor to help the career woman understand relationships between recognized Sun Signs and a host of personal and career problems. And she offers specific ways for dealing with conflicts, and such specific problems as: When is the best time to make a job switch?

THE CLAIRVOYANT
By Hans Holzer

PRICE: $2.25 T51573
CATEGORY: Novel (Hardcover publisher:
Mason/Charter 1976)

The story of a beautiful young Viennese girl whose
gift of prophecy took her from the mountains of
Austria to the glittering drawing rooms of Beverly
Hills. She began to exhibit psychic powers at the
age of four. Terrified of their daughter's "gift," her
parents sent her to a remote school. As she moved
from school to school and then from man to man,
she used her psychic abilities to climb to perilous
heights of fame and success!

Author of the best-selling
Murder In Amityville

DISPOSABLE PEOPLE
By Marshall Goldberg, M.D.
(Author of Critial List)
and Kenneth Kay

PRICE: $2.25 BT51574
CATEGORY: Novel (Original)

The ultimate thriller, in which today's medical and political morality determines for millions—who shall live and who shall die!

A disease more horrifying than the Black Plague rages out of control. In a mighty effort to contain it, Dr. Noah Blanchard is assigned by the President to head the Epidemic Task Force. When the hard choices have to be made, doctors and politicians are forced into a sinister plot to choose the "Disposable People."

SEND TO: **TOWER PUBLICATIONS**
P.O. BOX 270
NORWALK, CONN. 06852

PLEASE SEND ME THE FOLLOWING TITLES:

Quantity	Book Number	Price

IN THE EVENT THAT WE ARE OUT OF STOCK ON ANY OF YOUR SELECTIONS, PLEASE LIST ALTERNATE TITLES BELOW:

Postage/Handling

I enclose...

FOR U.S. ORDERS, add 50c for the first book and 10c for each additional book to cover cost of postage and handling. Buy five or more copies and we will pay for shipping. Sorry, no C.O.D.'s.

FOR ORDERS SENT OUTSIDE THE U.S.A., add $1.00 for the first book and 25c for each additional book. PAY BY foreign draft or money order drawn on a U.S. bank, payable in U.S. ($) dollars.

☐ **PLEASE SEND ME A FREE CATALOG.**

NAME_____
(Please print)

ADDRESS_____

CITY_____**STATE**_____**ZIP**_____
Allow Four Weeks for Delivery